OUT of MIND

OUT of MIND

Everest Avalanche
and a Barefoot Running Recovery

Joe French

SANDSTONE PRESS

First published in Great Britain in 2023 by
Sandstone Press Ltd
PO Box 41
Muir of Ord
IV6 7YX
Scotland

www.sandstonepress.com

ISBN: 978-1-914518-32-4
ISBNe: 978-1-914518-33-1

Sandstone Press is committed to a sustainable future.

This product is made of material from well-managed FSC®-certified forests, recycled materials, and other controlled sources. FSC® helps take care of forests for future generations.

Cover design by Nathan Ryder
Typeset by Biblichor Ltd, Scotland
Printed and bound by CPI Group (UK) Ltd, Croydon CR0 4YY

For Julie, Imogen and Jemima
. . . and Ziggy

CONTENTS

LIST OF ILLUSTRATIONS

All photographs author's own unless otherwise stated:

1. Dave MacLeod on the first free ascent of *Don't Die of Ignorance* X11, 11. Ben Nevis,
2. Andrew Greig sings *Wild Mountain Thyme* at Julie and Joe's wedding, 2008
3. Julie French on honeymoon in Tiree.
4. Filming from the Mittellegi Ridge, Eiger summit in background, 2013. Photo credit: Brian Hall
5. Everest Geography from Pumori Base Camp, 2014
6. Heavily laden porter heads to BC, 2014
7. Andy Tyson's Solar Power System and the NBC Rig, 2014
8. My friend and guide Andy Tyson, Everest Base Camp, 2014. Photo credit: Ed Wardle
9. Ed Wardle and Jonathon Fierro report live from Base Camp after the avalanche, 2014
10. Avalanche path. Photo credit: Rob Smith
11. Drinks at Adventure Consultants Puja ceremony, 2015
12. Adventure Consultants' camp before avalanche – dining tent, media tent and kitchen tent behind (yellow roof), 2015
13. Ground Zero. Dining tent (left frame), kitchen tent table (middle frame), media tent destroyed, 2015

PROLOGUE

EVEREST BASE CAMP

25th April 2015

A wave of animal prickles swept across my skin. My senses knew something that my mind did not. The ice beneath my feet juddered, then cracked and hissed. I swayed as if I was at sea. Then it stopped.

I looked up to see a figure running from the Icefall towards Base Camp and grabbed for my camera. A deep, thunderous roar began to echo all around. It was impossible to locate, but it was growing louder, as if the mountains were collapsing above me. As I found my frame, I noticed the same figure turning 180° and running back the way he came. I hit record and panned round.

The low grey cloud hanging above Base Camp began to expand violently. What the hell was I filming? Explosions of snow, ice, rock and debris, all churning together into one enormous blast right over our camp. I was so mesmerised by my shot, for a moment it didn't seem real. Then it burst out of my frame into reality. Instinctively I started to run, though it was pointless. The glacier was bare. There was nowhere to hide.

My camera was still rolling as I looked back over my shoulder. I heard myself cry out, unable to believe what I saw. Base Camp was disappearing under a dark shroud, expanding ever upwards and outwards. Within seconds the fierce shock wave had hit me and I was blown off my feet. As I crouched over my camera, something screamed past my head, and I braced myself for impact. This was it. Breathe, focus, breathe. I cut the camera, gasping and choking among howling waves of snow, ice and grit.

I was swallowing the mountain and it was expanding into my lungs, throat and nose. Beginning to suffocate, I didn't know if my eyes were open or closed. All I could see were white fuzzy dots, grey fuzzy dots, everywhere and in everything. My mind was ablaze with a million thoughts all at once. I wasn't ready to die. But I had to be brave, I had to die well. But my girls, my girls. How could this be happening?

1

RUNNING MAN 1: BAREFOOT BEGINNINGS

2020

I still feel self-conscious as I hobble across the gravel to the forest and the start of my run, despite this being the fifth year of my daily practice. The need to wear shoes outside is so ingrained that I can't help but feel like a weirdo by not doing so. This is amplified when sometimes, if the weather is particularly wild, I choose to leave the house in nothing more than a pair of swimming shorts. I hope no one is driving past on the single-track road that I must cross before I'm hidden among the trees. It would be a perfectly normal scene to witness in Colorado, but here in the wet wild west of Scotland, I have seen looks of horror and disbelief from the windows of cars happening to pass by just as I emerge.

The initial shock of stepping outside half naked into a raging storm brings out a gasp and the internal question: is this really necessary? Our sheep dog, Ziggy, who tends to hide under the trampoline in such conditions, doesn't seem to think so. Usually keen for a run, he's keeping his head down, pretending to ignore me.

I see the hairs on my chest rise and curl, trying to trap in any heat they can, and feel an explosion of goose-pimples race across my skin. Inhaling deeply through my nose, I focus on this breath. Pushing my diaphragm firmly down, I turn the bad postural hunch of my climber's shoulders up and out and try to stand tall, despite the urge to cower. 'Come on boy.' I exhale and with a huff, Ziggy stretches and ventures out. The woodland portal is waiting and soon we will disappear through it.

The change of atmosphere inside is dramatic. The lash of the rain is banished by the spiralling spruce above and the blustery air is muted and made sweet with fresh citrus and pine. I fill my lungs and curl my toes down into the soft mulch to ready them for what's ahead. They're in for a treat, for inside these damp depths a remarkable transformation has taken place. Undisturbed for decades by pollution or people, this once sterile spruce plantation has become home to a rich kingdom of moss and lichen. Free to creep and bloom and swell and weave a pristine mosaic of patchwork quilts over trees and ground and roads and ruins, this psychedelic playground truly is a barefoot runner's paradise. Shin-deep hummocks of pink sphagnum lie waiting to tempt my toes while wizards' beards of sage green whisper from branches as I prepare myself for launch.

My journey through the forest starts along a bowling alley of high banked moss. It encourages a side-to-side bounce rather than a run and is the perfect way to get going. Like a poorly bowled ball bouncing off the guards in the gutter, I am slow and steady, getting my feet and mind adjusted to the environment. I'm feeling the texture and temperature of the forest floor and loosening myself to its tone, before I become fully tuned in and can tentatively increase my pace. Once I can feel my movements come together into a steady, unified rhythm, I start my forest flow.

The spruce trees have been planted in regimented raised lines, crisscrossed with drainage ditches that need hopping and jumping over. My toes turn into claws that rip hungrily into crusts of moss as I leap, revealing roots underneath. Sometimes, I must

4

duck immediately into a low stoop as I land to avoid any branches at eye level that the deer may have missed as they foraged this track. This is no normal way to run. At times all four of my limbs are in contact with the forest floor, combining all sorts of muscle groups to allow my contortions through the trees to continue unimpeded.

Running like this requires a high level of focus and concentration. An overindulgence in thought can have painful consequences, but this is precisely why I love it so much. It is when one thought consumes me, and I become more involved with my internal dialogue than my external world, that I will make a mistake and slam my heel into an awkward tree root or cut my sole on a random stick. Whether they are thoughts of elation or despair, the result is the same, and I'm reminded of my lack of focus with a sharp bite from a fang of the forest.

So, I need to be in a different space. A space somewhere between those two extremes where mindful meditation can merge with instinctive intuition to guide me silently and safely through the trees. When I get it right, it feels majestic. Deliberate and precise as I can be, aiming for perfection in each step, completely flowing in body and by consequence, out of mind.

It is this need to get out of mind that brings me here. I've not always run in this forest. My first exploratory trips were ones of hunched introspection. Consumed so fully with traumatic thoughts rewinding and replaying again and again in my mind's eye, I barely noticed anything outside of me.

It was early summer 2015 and I had just returned home from a filming trip to Everest Base Camp for Raw TV. For the second year in a row, I had found myself in the midst of complete disaster. Nepal had been torn apart by a 7.8Mw earthquake. Around nine thousand people had died, with hundreds of thousands left injured or homeless. Countless ancient temples had crumbled to dust and whole villages had been swept away or buried by landslides. A huge avalanche was triggered above Everest Base Camp, killing twenty-two people, some within a few feet of me. It was the biggest single disaster ever to unfold on Everest.

The horror of the event was still pumping hard though my system weeks after my return to Scotland. I desperately needed grounding. The joy of returning home to the loving arms of my family was beyond measure. They were my buffer as I crashed back down to earth and the reality of my day to day. Despite their unlimited love and support, I still found myself feeling somewhat alone, just as I was alone when I struggled to gasp what I thought might be my last breath at Everest Base Camp. Only I knew what was going around in my head, and it wasn't pretty. I didn't know whether to talk about it or not, and almost felt under pressure to have the breakdown I sensed those around me were expecting. I found myself retreating to this same forest but having a completely different experience. I was wearing my shoes and a frown, more detached from the outside world than I'd ever been.

At first I had tried to numb myself with alcohol, but that didn't work. It took the edge off things, but in the middle of the night my demons would sober up and plague me as I slept, leaving me feeling even worse by the morning. Weed didn't help either. It just made me think more. I needed something else. Something that could bring me back down to earth. Something that could create a space between me and the constant torment of my thoughts.

I would find myself standing in the supermarket, locked in a silent battle, unable to decide what snacks to buy for my girls. It would appear to anyone passing that I was taking my time choosing between Oreos or Hobnobs. But in my mind, I was seeing blood and biscuits mashed together in an icy pulp. If I recognised anyone, I would stuff the packets back on the shelf and leave the aisle empty handed. I couldn't cope with small talk. I didn't want anyone to ask me how I was. I didn't want anyone to see me.

I was offered counselling by Raw TV but wasn't brave enough to take it. I was afraid to admit my struggles to myself, let alone anyone else. I didn't think anyone else could possibly understand how I was feeling. I'd heard about post-traumatic stress and post-traumatic stress disorder. But that was for soldiers, not producers. At first, I didn't understand what the difference was between them. I was scared of finding out, fearful of the label it could give me. I wasn't sure what was worse, not knowing what was wrong or being stigmatised by a label if I did? Disorder is such a negative word and implies so much. I didn't want that to be me. I still don't. I was a father and a husband and a successful TV producer/director. I had to get on with it. I had to be strong. Even now, I feel vulnerable admitting this. But my GP explained it *was* likely that I was experiencing post-traumatic stress. It could be expected in the short term, as the mind processed the trauma. If symptoms persisted and began to interfere with everyday life, post-traumatic stress would become post-traumatic stress disorder. Was that what was happening to me? Had my stress crossed a line and become a disorder? If so, why wasn't it affecting me all the time?

I don't know. I still haven't had any professional counselling. Instead, in between work and parenting, I have remained mostly among the trees and the moss, tuning into nature, trying to make sense of it all. Writing this book is a result of that. Getting my thoughts in order on these pages rather than jumbled up in my head, has been a helpful process. There has been a lot to ponder. Was my mental state simply due to the cumulative effects of the previous two years? Or did it have something to do with mountaineering, the highs and lows we all experience doing this most dangerous of sports? Or at the end of the day was it just me?

2

DON'T DIE OF IGNORANCE

I had already had an experience of extreme mental turbulence, long before I went to Everest. It had been triggered by another traumatic event in the mountains. Then, it resulted in a strange case of post-traumatic joy rather than stress and was also a little closer to home.

In February 2008 I was dating a local girl by the name of Julie Carver and things had been going well between us. She was working as an assistant producer for Hand Pict Productions in Edinburgh, while I was figuring out what do next with my life in Fort William. A petite and powerful nature girl, with freckled skin that glowed golden at the first hint of sunshine, she was most at home among trees or surfing the seas. Her blue-green eyes sparkled with fun every time we met and, even though I felt I was fighting above my weight, I really hoped this could be the start of something special.

Julie had enjoyed my first climbing film – a documentary about the history of rock climbing in Glen Nevis – which she had seen at a climbing festival in Edinburgh. I had teamed up with my friends John Sutherland, Ali Berardelli and Ed Grindley to produce it. We called ourselves Heather Hat after the obvious overhanging boulder in Glen Nevis, and set up a make shift edit suite in the upstairs of the old nursery in Roy Bridge. The fact that we didn't have a clue what we were doing didn't matter: it felt exciting and fresh. Even if we had to wait patiently for the toddler groups to finish and pack away each evening before we could start work.

Through making this film, I met the legend that was Dave MacLeod and we hit it off well. He was living in Dumbarton at the time and had just finished climbing his *Rhapsody* project, the first climb with the whopping grade E11 in the country, or anywhere in the world for that matter. Dave needed new challenges and it wasn't long before he and his wife Claire moved up to Lochaber. To facilitate his expanding adventures, the two of them somehow squeezed themselves into a studio apartment next to the Spar shop in Claggan. Not the most exotic place for one of the world's leading climbers, but Dave and Claire were keeping it real. It was the perfect place for Dave to launch his assault on Glen Nevis and he wasted little time in doing so, creating some classic climbs in the process. It was great to witness such an explosion of climbing in the Glen. Although, lost in the grand solitude of the place, you would have never even have known he was there.

One project in particular was a big one: *Don't Die of Ignorance*. The name referred to the notorious public health campaign at the time, warning of the dangers of AIDS. It was a climb Dave had been attempting on the North Face of Ben Nevis for four consecutive years and had fallen at the same spot each time. The route had already been climbed in winter by Andy Cave and Simon Yates in 1987, but they had used several points of aid* to get through the outrageously hard traverse on the first pitch, which was the crux of the whole climb. Dave's plan was to climb this

---

* Aid climbing is a style of climbing in which standing on or pulling oneself up via devices attached to fixed or placed protection is used to make upward progress.

route free. His only protection would be the gear that he placed as he climbed. If he somehow managed to achieve this, it would be the hardest technical climbing ever achieved on Ben Nevis and Britain's hardest mixed route to date.

Dave is one of the world's most gifted all-round climbers, excelling at the top level whether it be on a boulder, sport route or mountain cliff. I, on the other hand, am not. After enthusiastically accepting the opportunity to join him with my camera, my limitations became apparent to me in the most serious of ways.

I was buzzing as John Sutherland, Claire MacLeod, Dave and I stomped up to the CIC* hut in military style. I was a smoker back then and managed to get a quick roll-up prepared and puffed without breaking stride. However, my casual excitement gradually began to dissipate, and by the time we had reached the hut, it had u-turned into utter terror. Bang in the middle of Corrie Na Ciste was *Don't Die of Ignorance* looming at the crest of a fierce tidal wave of granite. It seemed to be screaming its name as a warning to me. Or was that the wind? The line of the route went up the middle of the Comb Buttress and was the most obvious, imposing and direct way up the whole of the North Face. I looked at John for reassurance but didn't find any. His friendly face looked more serious than usual. I could see he was thinking the same as me. With a raise of his eyebrows and a nervous grin, John looked away and shook his head. Should I bail now? Could I bail now? What was I doing? Could another quick roll-up help?

I looked at Dave, who was beaming. 'What you reckon, Joe? Still keen?' I tried to hide the distinct tremble in my hand as I attempted to roll this, the most important of roll-ups. It was as

---

* Charles Inglis Clark – the hut was erected in memory of this climber, killed in WW1.

if he could read my mind or at least knew that as soon as I saw the reality of his proposition, I might have second thoughts. This was to be our first climb together after all. 'Wow,' I responded, but the wind sucked my little word away before it had left my mouth and it cartwheeled off into the snow.

I glanced back up at our route and wished I hadn't. The huge tombstone of granite was looking more menacing and impenetrable by the minute. Spindrift curled wildly over the summit cornices like smoke from a dragon's nose and my mouth was so dry I could have struck a match in it. I eventually allowed my eyes to fix with Dave's; his were full of intense enquiry. 'So?' he asked. I looked down at my failed roll-up and crumpled the soggy Rizla and tobacco in my fist. 'Britain's hardest route?' I heard myself ask. 'Fucking let's 'ave it.' And that was that.

I became increasingly subdued as we continued up into the corrie to commence our climb. As Dave started getting himself clipped in, psyched up and sorted, I could barely tie into my own rope – or speak, for that matter. The first pitch was the crux to the whole climb. He needed to traverse an awful looking undercut crack that rose and snaked horizontally away from our ledge for about twenty metres towards a blunt prow that jutted out into space. It was just wide enough to wedge your foot in, but other than that I couldn't see any foot holds or ice that were thick enough to make it worthwhile swinging my axe. This was my first taste of hard mixed climbing and already I felt sick.

'Climb when ready, Dave!'

Dave set off, stepping straight out into space and tip-toeing his tiny metal toes across non-existent footholds. The odd nub of granite was just big enough to bear some of his weight. Everything sloped the wrong way and there were no holds or features anywhere, other than the icy crack that he followed. Dave had to turn his axes upside down so that their shafts stuck up and out of the crack rather than down and from it and use them as teetering levers to crank down on, in the hope they wouldn't rip out. This technique is known as 'tin opening' and I'd never seen anything like it before in my life. He looked like a giant space crab as he scuttled along the crack with his metal pincers, yellow helmet and red jacket. I stood open mouthed with a mixture of amazement and terror at what I was finding myself witness to.

'Go on, Dave! Send it!' I shouted at the twitching ropes as they snaked out of sight, pleased with the positive tone of my voice. I didn't really think he would do it this time. Pretty soon we could be back home with a nice cup of tea, and we could pretend this never happened. I could see John way below on the corrie floor lying back in the snow, camera pressed to his face. I was cold on a snow ledge and dancing on the spot to warm myself up. Dave was taking some time. I sang Bob Marley's *Three Little Birds* to myself in the hope that it would banish the rising terror in my system and bring about a sense of calm. It didn't. I was worried about everything and seriously doubting whether every little thing would be all right.

My impromptu performance was brought to an abrupt end when I heard Dave screaming. His voice was thin and urgent, but at best muffled, at worst completely inaudible through the buffering wind. He was at the crux move and needed slack. This was it, the point of no return. I needed to be on it here like never before. He was about to commit his life to pushing through the boundaries of what was thought possible, and I was holding his ropes. *Oh no.* They were iced up and heavy, hard to manage as the fear inside me. If I gave him too much slack he could have a nasty fall, but if I didn't give him enough, I could pull him off the cliff.

I don't know if it was better or worse that he was obscured from my view at this point, but his screams for slack were getting louder, accompanied now by primal sounding grunts. With so much drag and ice on the ropes it was almost impossible to let them run free. This would only get worse once he left the traverse and started climbing vertically. A small group of onlookers had gathered at the corrie floor, seemingly miles beneath our route and were craning their necks to see what I could not.

As Dave reached the crux, the sliver of rock providing the tiny dinks for his feet got smaller and smaller until they disappeared and there were no footholds left at all, just hundreds of feet of space between him and the boulders below. This was the crux to the whole route. With one last scream, Dave entered some elevated state and launched into the unknown. He tried desperately to gain his balance, but because of the lack of holds, it was impossible for him to find any way of doing this. The only option left available to him was to cut loose and hang by his right hand on the upturned shaft of his axe, as it slowly slid out of the icy crack. Miraculously it held long enough to get his left hand on as well, but now he was hanging by both hands off this one precariously positioned axe.

Dave's centre of gravity shifted as soon as he got his left hand on, so he was able to find a way to use his feet on the tiniest of edges. This gave him enough balance to continue this ground-breaking sequence. With the utmost composure, he took his other axe off his shoulder where it had been balancing and started scratching around with it for the next holds in the icy wall above. He karate kicked his legs round in one last masterly display of control and seated his right foot precisely where it needed to be – on a rib of rock that allowed him to regain his balance and continue his journey upwards and into the unknown.

The crux was in the bag, but it was far from over. He now had to climb a blank ten-metre wall with the rope drag at critical level. Axes were ripping and feet slipping wildly as he continued upwards, screaming, going for broke as if his life depended on it. And it did. With each move up, the rope would do its best to drag him back down and I was doing my best not to whimper at the intensity of the moment. Inch by inch, move by move, he continued his triumphant conquest upwards until finally I heard the words, 'That's me safe, Joe,' echo down from the icy amphitheatre above. For a moment I felt relief, then terror.

3

SPACE CRAB

My new reality hit me hard. History was only half made, and the pressure was now on me to follow. I was already shaking. I could not climb the way Dave had; it was much too hard. Usually when climbing second, you can follow the rope directly upwards to the lead climber. They can keep it nice and tight and even help you through the hard parts with an extra hard tug if required. This wasn't the case here. As this pitch was a traverse, the rope was loosely snaking away from me in a horizontal direction and Dave could give me no assistance from above.

The only option for me was to aid across, placing the picks of my axes through the karabiners attached to the protection he had left behind. This had seemed a perfectly reasonable plan when we had gone through it all during our walk in, but now it was a different proposition altogether. My nerves were in tatters after standing cold and alone on that ledge for I don't know how long. The whole time my mind had been fluctuating between wanting him to succeed and secretly hoping he wouldn't so that we could go home.

All that was irrelevant now. My only option was to take a deep breath and launch myself out into space in pursuit of this climbing genius and follow in his non-existent footsteps. There was no easy way to get moving. I paced and muttered and flapped my arms for at least twenty minutes before I felt psyched up enough

15

to dive in. When I eventually did, I was out of my depth within the first move.

To place a crampon onto the tiniest of edges requires a great deal of skill, composure and a confidence that it will hold firm when you move. I had none of this and, as this was my first serious mixed route, it was an appalling place to try and learn. With my brain misfiring and unsure quite what to do, I put my left axe through the closest karabiner to me in the crack while I was still on the belay ledge, which was easy enough. I then lowered my weight onto this axe and allowed my feet to scrape and skid at the wall, eventually finding enough friction to make the next move possible. I pulled myself back up high on this left axe and, at full stretch, managed to find the next karabiner with my right axe out along the crack. For the briefest of moments this felt like progress. I had two solid holds and I was holding them. How hard can this be? All I had to do was ooch along like this and the climb would be in the bag.

Unfortunately, it wasn't that simple. In my hasty and anxious plan to launch out along these loops, I'd neglected to pay enough attention to my feet and think through exactly how I planned to move along the crack once I was in it. Now I was wholly committed with my arms at full stretch, feet scraping wildly at nothing. I desperately looked down for something, but all I could see was the void I was hanging over. Now I was the space crab with my pincers pulled apart. Pump and fatigue started to build in my arms. I became rigid on my axes, as if I was in the clutches of an electric shock. I was unable to move forward or back, unable to find any holds for my feet or any way of making another move. I was also acutely aware that there was no one but myself who could help me get me out of this situation. Time started slowing and stretching around me. I had to do something, but what?

With tremendous effort I managed to get my left foot up and onto a hold, so at least I now had three points of contact. It was progress and I breathed and prayed. But my right foot was still dangling in space. As all my weight was now hanging off my axes, there was no way I could flick them up and out of the karabiners. The ropes between us were slack on my harness. They gave no help at all. I needed to come up with a plan, and quick. The only solution I could see was to pull as hard as I could on my left axe in the hope that with enough force, I could rip out the gear Dave had placed and free one of my arms. This was by no means guaranteed as Dave would have been sure to have placed his gear very well and once it is in, it can be very tricky, if not impossible, to get out.

I had no choice. I pulled and pulled desperately on my axe and pushed down against my left leg as hard as I could. Oh, please God, set me free! Eventually, with one ginormous heave, the gear and my axe ripped out of the crack and flew towards my face, narrowly missing me. My situation had taken a huge turn for the worse.

As I ripped the gear out on my left, all my weight swung violently onto my right axe and all I could do was clutch desperately to this. For a few seconds I managed to hold a one arm lock off, but this didn't last long and slowly I sank and slipped down the shaft of my axe towards oblivion. My mouth burned dry with acid and my vision became patchy. I knew there was one more inevitable part of this process still to go. How long could I possibly hold onto the axe? The lactic acid in my arm was throbbing with a pump so powerful it was prising my fingers apart. I tried in vain to do a one arm pull up, but no chance. My legs bicycled through empty space, and it all became too much. I let go of the axe and my situation took yet another terrifying turn for the worse.

So as not to drop and lose my axes while climbing, I had leashes on them that attached to my wrist. My full weight was now hanging off this leash while the pick of the axe remained tightly in the karabiner. The leash was biting hard into my wrist. My helpless legs kicked frantically at nothing. I started to lose sensation in my hand. My wrist joint was being simultaneously stretched and crushed by two opposing forces running through it. The harder I pulled, the tighter it got, first pins and needles, then numbness. Then nothing. My dead weight hung over the void, and I now couldn't feel my hand. My legs continued to pedal through thin air. Curtains started to close on my vision. Primal fear was stretching and playing with time. This moment had become an eternity that was no longer linked to the next moment, just a series of patchy images. Was it even my hand I was looking at?

At this point I felt a profound shift of perspective occur. I became a witness to my situation rather than the person it was happening to. Not from out of my body, but from somewhere else within. Then came an explosion of strength and clarity that surged through my system, as if I had blown through my own seams to a place beyond fear. I was able to see my situation objectively and come up with a plan.

I had a jumar on the back of my harness (a clampy device used to ascend ropes) and managed to reach round to carefully unclip it. I held it in my trembling hand as if it was the most precious object in the world. Next, with this hand and my teeth, I managed to open its spiky jaws and very carefully place it as high up on the rope above me as I could manage. This was it. One shot before God knows what kind of recovery mission would be needed to get my hanging body out of this mess.

I breathed and focused. I heaved down on the jumar and somehow managed a one arm pull up for the first and only time in my life. I held it while battling against the stretch of the rope and the extra weight from my rucksack and somehow stayed locked off on it. Then, with this new wobbly height gain, I was able to flick my right axe free from the karabiner it had been stuck through and bingo, I was free. My weight came crashing back down onto the ropes and I hung in space in a tangle of exhaustion.

There was no time to dwell on my relief. Dave had no clue what had been going on as I had been obscured from his view by the overhang. His shouts had remained unanswered as I had nothing intelligible or encouraging to offer. I could hear only one word in three anyway because of the hassling wind. I was now hanging in space with the ropes and axes tangled together in a dreadful knot around my harness. He was huddled up in a ball at the belay, becoming dangerously cold.

We were climbing on twin 7.8mm ropes, too thin to ever climb on one alone, but together they created enough strength to take a fall safely. This helped to minimise rope drag when the route changed directions. My heart sank to new depths when I realised that because of the two differing directions of the rope, I had to do something that I really didn't want to do. One of the ropes led to Dave straight above me, while the other one led diagonally up and rightwards towards the crack above me. I had only one option. I had to untie one of the ropes. I shouted Dave and John in the hope that they could hear me and give some advice, but the wind was wild and their responses indistinct. I was alone.

In trembling silence, I figured out which rope was which. My hand fumbled with the tight figure-of-eight knot until it loosened sufficiently. It was hard to do this because my weight was still on it. Carefully I then untied it, trying to be as still as possible. I could hear my concentrated breath as I held the end of rope, feeling its pull towards the crack. I let it go and began to swoop silently through the air until I was directly beneath Dave, some fifty metres above me at the belay. Thank God it was the right one. But again, no time to rejoice. I looked up and saw how precarious my situation now was. The thin sliver of pink nylon I was hanging by rubbed tightly against the jagged lip of the black overhang. If my movements now were too forceful or jerky, the cliff's sharp fangs would surely bite through and sever this final lifeline.

I began the most terrifying and delicate jumar of my life. Creeping gently up the rope, barely allowing myself to breathe, I began to make progress. Time continued to bend and wobble. I couldn't bear to look up at the rope as it heaved and rubbed on the razor edge of granite, but there was no choice. Each time I raised the jumar, I automatically raised my head and prayed. As I was still hanging in space, all my weight was on this rope and each time I pulled I knew it could be my last heave. If it did twang, that would be that. I would fall hundreds of metres to the corrie floor and be smashed to pieces.

Miraculously, the rope continued to remain strong and inch by inch I crept higher until I was able to get my feet back on the buttress and the angle eased. Eventually, a slumped heap of red Gore-Tex came into view at the belay, and I staggered up through the snow towards it.

Dave didn't look good. He was huddled in the foetal position over the ropes. Blue lips, face opaque and so cold he'd gone beyond shivering – a classic sign that he was dangerously hypothermic. Because the climbing was so difficult, he'd dropped a layer of clothing and was wearing nothing but his thermals, outer shell and a very thin pair of gloves. He also had a limited rack of gear with him, to minimise weight. This gamble was now being put to the test as he was clearly used to climbing with slicker partners than me.

Dave was still pleased to see me when I arrived, for a few moments at least. I gave him my down jacket and rubbed his legs frantically, while congratulating him and trying to explain what had happened to me. He cut through my manic babbles with one deadpan question. 'Where is all the gear, Joe?' Our hearts sank. Because I had untied the rope and climbed directly to Dave, I had bypassed all the gear that was in and around the crack. We now needed this gear to protect the next two hundred metres or so of extreme climbing still in front of us. 'Sorry dude,' was all I could offer, and I rubbed his legs a little harder to compensate.

Dave's ability to control his emotions in this most serious of situations was as impressive as the climbing skills that he had to put us there in the first place. He now stepped up and took control with great calmness and composure and I loved him for that. Once I was safe and he was warm, he abseiled back down to the crack, retrieved all the gear and returned to me as if we were just starting out. A superhuman effort from a truly superhuman being. I only found out later that he had severe frostnip in his fingers at this point which resulted in numbness and poor circulation for a whole year afterwards.

We still had six pitches of hard climbing left ahead of us but now, as the crux was in the bag, nothing was going to stop us from completing this climb. Well, at least that's what I hoped. I had one more confession to make. Somehow in my haze of excitement that morning, I had forgotten to put my head-torch in my bag. I saw Dave's lip curl slightly when I mentioned this, but once again he stayed calm and resisted the urge to scream at me. I must have been the worst climbing partner he'd ever had!

Twilight soon came and we still had a long way to go. When the terrain allowed, we would move together so Dave could talk me through the moves and shine his torch back toward me to illuminate my route. At one point he had to give me his iPhone and I was climbing by the dim light from the screen to help me.

This was in the days before phones had torches. Pitches somehow passed and progress was made but, as we continued our ascent, Dave was increasingly concerned about one final tricky section that still lay ahead. It was a pitch of grade V6 which I would have to climb in the dark. As I stood belaying and watching his torch light move further away from me, I was pretty concerned myself.

Dave shouted, 'Climb when ready,' and with a deep breath I started my dark scratchings. Just then, a giant's breath of wind parted the clouds and flooded the mountain in bright moonlight. Success was guaranteed. We whooped with joy as we topped out among thin wisps of silver and soft mushrooms of snow. History had been made. Dave had realised his dream of free climbing *Don't Die of Ignorance* and gave it the whopping grade of X11, 11. The hardest mixed climb in Britain at the time.

4

TURBULENT TIMES

I had survived the route, but what about the aftermath? I didn't sleep much that night, just enough to rest my limbs, but not enough to slow down the adrenaline and endorphins still pumping hard through my system. Julie was back in Edinburgh and oblivious to my adventure – all she knew was that I was going climbing and it was probably a good job I left it at that. Meanwhile, the potent mix of near death and new love bubbled and fizzed like champagne in my veins. I felt euphoric as I bounded round my house in my boxer shorts. We had done it! History had been made! I had survived! Laughing out loud at the craziness of the previous day's events, I was playing air guitar as I put my clothes on and headed out to work.

My friend Bruno Berardelli had recently given me a job at his Highland Wood Energy business, just outside Fort William. Judging by the perplexed looks on my colleagues' faces as I burst into the office that morning, I should perhaps have taken the day off. It was hard to articulate my words as I garbled through the previous day's events. Dave's brilliance, my buffoonery, hanging by one arm, having to untie my rope. My day at work didn't seem like an important subject at all. 'Are you all right, Joe?' Bruno asked. He sat back in his smart blue shirt and clicked his pen between his fingers. I bounced off the walls around him, 'Yeah mate, isn't it great to be alive!'

I then left the office to get some supplies from Plumbline and reversed the work van straight into a parked vehicle outside the shop. I drove off none the wiser, whistling and waving to the witnesses as I went on my merry way.

What followed was one of the strangest weeks at work I'd ever had. There was a wood-chip boiler needing serviced on the Isle of Mull and, as I set off with my colleague Victor Johnston, I still hadn't managed to get any sleep. Even though I must have been close to the point of collapse, I couldn't switch off and come down from the state of elation I was experiencing. The surge of strength and clarity I'd felt on the mountain had stayed with me, but now back on solid ground, I was struggling to know how to handle it. I could still feel its charge swirling in my stomach. It was impossible to focus on anything else and my conversation was all over the place. 'Sure you're all right to drive, young man?' Victor asked as we approached the Mull ferry. I was babbling about life, death, and the universe while his right knee bounced up and down, feet braking on thin air. 'Just keep your eyes on the road, please!'

I eventually hit a brick wall mid-week, but thankfully I wasn't driving at the time. Victor had found an article in his Daily Record about our ascent of *Don't Die*. 'Blimey Joe, have you seen this?' He chuckled, cigarette smoke unwinding around him. 'You guys are famous!' I was crouching uncomfortably under a boiler, covered in dirt, and trying to work with hands that hadn't stopped shaking since the climb. The combination of hearing this tabloid version of events, along with the rather mundane task at hand was too much for me. Much to Victor's horror, I passed out in a heap of exhaustion next to a box of spare parts.

That evening I went for a drive to chill out and get some space. But far from finding a sense of calm, I ended up feeling even more excited when a sea eagle swooped in front of the van. Its huge wings glided in front of me for a good mile or so in the direction of Calgary Bay. In my heightened state, I felt as if this magnificent bird was some sort of shamanic sign, leading me in the right direction for some big changes I wanted to make in my life. The Beatles' *Across the Universe* was playing as I soared along, towards the setting sun. The grin on my face was wide enough to make my cheeks hurt. I sat and watched visions of white horses in the waves and clouds from the grassy tufts above Calgary Bay. Chanting *Aum* vigorously, I felt blissful and infinite as the sky turned pink around me.

I had been having a tricky time of things in the run up to the climb. Bruno had kindly given me the job at Highland Wood Energy as a steppingstone away from my role as Musician in Residence for Room 13 at Lochaber High School. I'd been working there for three years, transforming an old classroom into a recording studio for students to run as a business. With a vocal booth made from old church curtains, and posters of Buddha and Bob Marley on the walls, it was pretty ramshackle. Although most teachers were supportive, I sensed that some in the staffroom weren't impressed – especially when the drum and bass kicked in. I had become increasingly stressed and isolated, unsure about which direction to go with it. I hadn't wanted to let the project's founder, visionary artist Rob Fairley, or my students down, but years of making it up as I went along had been exhausting. I had run out of ideas and dance moves.

I'd also been having a crisis about what to do with my house in Fort William. I had bought it with Katrina Dexter, my girlfriend of nine years, but things hadn't worked out between us. We had grown apart since moving up from Sheffield and split up earlier that year. I was still living there, haunted by memories of a previous life.

Worst of all, my best friend and climbing partner, Damien Holmes, had recently been killed in the Alps. We had met back in 1999 while working at Firth Park School in Sheffield. I was a learning support assistant; he was a teacher. In class he'd often tease out a snort of laughter in me, as his deadpan jokes flew over the students' heads. When the bell rang at the end of the day, we would race out to the Peak District in his Peugeot 205, LTJ Bukum's *Logical Progression* banging out of the speakers. We would climb and boulder together until our fingers hurt, sometimes even managing one hundred short routes at Burbage Edge in one evening. At the weekends we would head down to Snowdonia, solo V-Diffs* in the rain, sleep under boulders and live like soggy kings.

He quit teaching to follow his dreams and had just qualified as an international mountain leader when he headed off to the Aiguille du Grépon for one last climb. I had received a text message from him the night before. He was buzzing. Next thing I had was his wife Ceri Aston on the other end of the phone. 'He's dead, Joe.' Damien had been killed instantly when a block of ice the size of a refrigerator landed on top of him. He was only thirty-four. I had been best boy and DJ at their wedding only three years before. Carrying his coffin was almost too much to cope with.

I was grateful to Bruno for giving me the job at Highland Wood Energy, but in the context of all this, I had started to feel trapped and was realising that I was far from living my dreams. I didn't want to be servicing boilers just to pay a mortgage on a house that I didn't want to be in. Where was the joy in that? The pressure that had been building up in my psyche had perhaps released itself among the intensity of *Don't Die*. I felt I had come down from the mountain liberated from this difficult period

---

* Climbs graded as Very Difficult.

with nothing but profound feelings of clarity, confidence and connection – not only to a greater force, but to everyone and everything around me. I still find it hard to articulate exactly how this manifested, but it was a physical feeling rather than an abstract thought.

Within weeks of that sunset at Calgary Bay, I quit my job, put my house on the market and proposed to Julie. It felt thrilling to embrace the intense feelings of love Julie and I shared, with no holding back. Committing to a life together felt like the easiest and most brilliant thing we could possibly do. We had a spontaneous spiritual marriage at Julie's family farm. Her parents, Chris and Siobhan Carver, threw rice over us and gave us their blessing. With a horseshoe lashed to the front of my Vauxhall Vectra, incense burning on the dashboard and Sister Sledge's *Lost in Music* on stereo cassette, we left for a new life in Edinburgh. Life couldn't possible have been any better. We married officially only seven months later, such was the intensity of our romance.

I was surfing waves of elation and had never felt anything like it in my life. I would wake as soon as the sun hit the sky, heart already pounding with excitement for the day. Up until the climb, I had always dressed scruffy – climbing trousers, a hoodie and Five Ten trainers. Now though, I wore an Indiana Jones style hat, dry-as-a-bone jacket and Spanish leather riding boots. This new era had obviously inspired a new look. I would talk to strangers as if they were friends and delve straight into heavy subject matter such as divine forces or the illusionary nature of existence. I felt completely liberated from self-consciousness or self-doubt. For a good while, I lived with absolutely no fear at all. Perhaps the sheer volume of it had saturated my system and I had become numb to its vibration.

While climbing Tower Ridge on Ben Nevis with John Sutherland and Bruno Berardelli a few weeks later, I was feeling particularly invincible. The crux of the route is called Tower Gap, where the knife edge ridge disappears completely. Climbers are forced into a delicate down climb at this point, then an exposed step across thin air. The gap is perhaps only one metre, but the surfaces of rocks on either side aren't level and one side is higher than the other. If you fall without a rope here, its highly likely you will die. Such was my state of mind that, despite it being a drizzly day, I leaped over the gap from a standing start. I landed on the other side with a bump and grabbed a pillar of rock to steady myself. I hadn't even stopped to take my rucksack off. In my mind I made the leap easily, but John and Bruno saw a distinct wobble when I landed on the far side. It makes me shiver to think I did this now, but at the time I didn't give it a second thought.

Eventually though, what goes up, comes down. I learned this later in the year as I crashed back down to earth on the streets of Edinburgh as a newly married, but unemployed man. The excitement of our wedding had died down and reality had kicked me hard. I needed to make a living. It was soon apparent how competitive the TV and film industry was. I was now a tiny fish in a big pond and was struggling to swim. What chance did I have?

Our train that was bound to glory from the station of *Don't Die* had become de-railed and I was out on foot asking for work on Marquee sites. I was struggling to keep positive, embarrassed by my predicament. I desperately wanted to prove my worth. Not just to Julie and her family, but to a world that I now felt more disconnected from than ever. Those joyful and profound feelings had completely disappeared. Instead, I was consumed with more self-doubt and introspection than I'd ever felt in my life. I started to slip towards depression and began to wonder and worry about my behaviour over the previous few months. Had my connection to that greater force been nothing more than a manic episode?

My stepfather Andrew Greig (more about him later) suggested that I spoke with a Buddhist friend of his called Edie Irwin. She was part of the fabric of Samye Ling Monastery here in Scotland, a qualified teacher of Tibetan medicine and an experienced psychotherapist. We met in a busy French café near Princes Street, where I was pleased to see that despite being a committed Buddhist, she still enjoyed a glass of red wine or two. She had bushy brown hair and wise eyes, and immediately made me feel at ease. So much so that I got stuck into a beer or two myself.

I explained my feelings of what I named 'Post-Traumatic Joy' in the aftermath of *Don't Die* and how I was struggling to remember those feelings, almost like they had all been experienced by someone else. She listened intently and held my gaze as she took a sip of her Bordeaux. 'It's okay to have your head in the clouds, Joe, but you must keep your feet on the ground at the same time.' What she helped me to realise was that my current feeling of lowness was nothing more than the rebound from my feeling of highness that I had experienced a few months before. While I embraced those feelings of extreme joy, I had also inadvertently created a void for a depression to sink into. Seemingly they were the reverse sides of the same coin. The trick, she suggested, was to find the middle path between those two extremes. This seemed like very sensible advice to me.

I also told her about my chanting of *Aum* and the pleasant vibrations I felt it generating within me. Edie looked slightly concerned at this. 'You need to stop doing so much of that for a start!' I wasn't expecting that response, especially from a Buddhist. I thought that's what they did? She went on to explain that this practice was likely to be creating an abundance of the space element in my system and it sounded to her like I already had plenty of that. As she polished off her glass, her smile was warm. 'You need to ground yourself instead, Joe. Have you ever tried gardening?' She assured me that I would feel the stabilising benefits of having my hands in the soil – and do you know what? She was right. But it wasn't until a few years later that I really felt the power of this simple remedy to be true.

5

RUNNING MAN 2:
LEARNING TO BREATHE

2020

Lasers of light penetrate the canopy, illuminating and punctuating moments of now, left behind in an instant as I continue my flow. This traverse of the trunks demands dynamic strides across soft half-pipes of mossy mulch. I'm running fast and feeling free. My breath is important as it sets the rhythm and tempo over the constantly changing terrain. I am aiming for conscious union between the two. As I breathe in, I do so through my nose with gentle but deliberate force, so my belly expands outwards. I give some attention to my solar plexus, the point at the pit of my stomach where all sorts of nerves join, before swiftly exhaling through my nose, contracting my stomach inwards and up.

This simple technique turns my diaphragm into some sort of internal wing. It helps me to glide along in my flow-like state for much longer periods of time. The longer it goes on, the more thrilling it becomes. Only when it is broken again do I realise just how powerful it is. It could be compared to whizzing down a hill on a mountain bike. The thing that makes you crash isn't necessarily the obstacle in your way, but your state of mind as you approach it.

I've spent time experimenting with different breathing techniques before settling on this one. I've even tried running without breathing at all. My ability to stay witness to the continuous succession of my thoughts is certainly affected when I lose conscious connection to my breath. It happens all the time. My thoughts seem to have different weights. Some are light and trivial, not strong enough to interfere with my main controls. Others are deeper and longer and harder to ignore. 'Follow me!' they shout, luring my attention, forcing a mistake, and leaving me with a sore foot. Some are so heavy they bring me to a complete standstill, leaving me rooted in the same place, staring blankly at trees. If this happens, I'm in the wrong headspace for barefoot running. I need to reset. The problem is, the more I try not to think about something, the more I think about it.

What helps me here is to extend my internal wing. I imagine the top of it is held by the tiny muscles inside my nostrils. They strengthen the more they are flexed and flared. It feels like a brand-new oxygen processing chamber has been created up there, powerful enough to make my forehead tingle at times. If I clear my nose and practise a few rounds of alternate nostril breathing (using my thumb and index finger), I feel the charge of the forest flowing in and over my thoughts, smoothing them down as I follow it round my system. Flexing my internal wing, the base of which is now my diaphragm, I pull the air down to my solar plexus where it swirls and fizzes as I begin to move. Slowly at first, but then with a swoop and a glide I find my way back into my rhythm, with my feet firmly on the ground. The solitude of the forest allows me to run like this. If I were surrounded by people, I would be aware of them, and the lens of my enquiry would lose focus. I couldn't just stop running in the middle of a street and stare into space because of a heavy thought. How weird would that be? But among the trees it is perfectly fine.

I mostly run at three-quarter speed, aiming to finish my run at the same pace that I started. This is the best way of maintaining the self-perpetuating intensity of my trance-like state, but if the terrain allows, I can never resist the exhilaration of a barefoot sprint. The buzz it generates is huge. My mouth remains tightly shut and my tongue rests at its roof, just behind my front teeth. This forms a closed circuit keeping me fully charged up through the trees. With every step, thousands of tiny sole receptors fire instantaneous messages to my subconscious self. If I do hit a stick, my brain will tell the surrounding muscle group to recoil or contract and prevent injury as much as it can. All without any conscious thought. Eons of evolution have made this possible and the more I'm in full flow, the more instinctive this action is. I become connected to my ancestral past. Joe, the vegetarian hunter-gatherer, running free in the forest – not on the hunt for food, but for a deeper understanding of my self.

I arrive at a pocket of native birch and must slow down, as the abrupt change in environment necessitates an adjustment in my stride. My core muscles absorb my speed in the same way the engine of our van does if I change straight from third to first gear. Among spruce, the floor is soft and for the most part spongy. In the bog of the birch, it is a different story. As these are native ancestors of an ancient forest, they have grown naturally and there is plenty of space between them for rough gnarls of Highland grass to grow. Extreme caution is needed here as black birch twigs hide like rotten fangs in these thick tufts, ready to bite at my feet. Here I must tip-toe and lurch, tuned in fully to the weight and force behind each foot placement.

A crumbled wall slumps through this native patch. Probably belonging to a crofter at some point, it has now been reclaimed by the forest. Moss has grown so thick and deep around it that the stones have disappeared completely. Now it has become a soft humpback bridge. As I cross it, my feet find their way into well-trodden grooves. The cool mud kisses my hot sole and I gain confidence to build up my pace again.

The precise angle of my foot is important as each landing effects the next take-off. Over the years I've created a mental map of where and how my foot should land in the same way I work out a sequence of moves when climbing a rock. If I am fully present, the micro adjustments happen automatically as I move through the air, between each foot strike, some of which are conscious and some of which are not.

This reminds me of a similar state I used to experience while solo climbing on the Gritstone Crags just outside Sheffield. Here I spent much teenage time learning the moves of many short climbs at Burbage Edge as if they were quotes from books. I would lie awake at night reciting them to myself, imagining my sleepy body moving through them. I can still remember some of them now – the awkward knee drop of *Banana Finger Direct* or the painful thumb sprag of *West Side Story*. I learned to read the rock like braille, remembering in detail the precise way to crimp my fingers on a crystal or smear my foot on a tiny edge. I also found out from painful experience the importance of mind control in the face of fear.

Hunters Bar and Nether Edge felt like the spiritual home of Sheffield climbing when I was growing up. It was the late 1980s and Alun Hughes's classic Johnny Dawes film, *Stone Monkey*, had just been released. My ten-year-old imagination was alive with adventure. The climbers themselves looked like an exotic tribe of Super Apes, hanging out mostly underground, training on steeply overhanging cellar boards when not climbing or partying in the Peak District. Through the black railings of Hunters Bar Middle School, it was easy for me to spot them in their bright lycra trousers, puffy down jackets and crusty dreadlocks. I'd see them hanging by their fingertips from bus shelters, looking to me full of mystery as they waited for the Eager Beaver bus to the Peak, a real bargain journey at just 7p a ride. I was desperate to get on board and journey into their world.

At High Storrs Secondary School a few years later, I got my chance. I'd been growing increasingly demotivated at school and soul-searching was my default setting. Home was split between two houses after my mum and dad's divorce. Despite their constant love and encouragement, it was hard for me to feel settled. I was sensitive to my dad's sadness and my mum's worry and felt responsible for my younger brother Joshua as we moved from house to house. The experience left me feeling old beyond my years, already witness to the fragilities of adult life. As a teenager I became increasingly resentful of any pressure to conform with rules or convention, when for me life didn't seem very conventional at all. I needed something to channel my creativity and energy into, beyond the walls of the classroom.

Enter Richard Haszko. I'd seen a photo of him in Joe Simpson's book *This Game of Ghosts*. He was wearing a curious outfit – a loose linen shirt, open to his chest, baggy Indian trousers and a flat hat that looked like two puffy pancakes. Next to the photo, the caption read 'Glorious Leader'. I couldn't quite believe it when this Glorious Leader walked into our classroom one afternoon, wearing John Lennon glasses and dressed as a relaxed supply teacher. I sidled up to him after the bell, full of awe and questions. 'So, you're friends with Joe Simpson, are you?' From that moment he became my friend too. He had me hanging off door frames to strengthen my fingers, lent me classic books such as Heinrich Harrer's *The White Spider* and even gave me his late friend Al Rouse's turquoise down jacket to keep me warm. I treasured it like a sacred robe.

Just seven minutes' drive from High Storrs School were the Gritstone edges of Burbage North. Once lessons were over,

Richard would swap his blackboard chalk for climbing chalk and teach me to climb. How I loved this vertical world he'd introduced me to. There were ethics as to how you climbed, rather than rules, and moving over rock gave me a new sense of freedom as I tried to make sense of my place on this planet. I soon started to spot the Super Apes of Hunters Bar out on the crags and finally felt I'd found my tribe. They were a mostly scruffy and friendly bunch with interesting names like Boggo and Grimer. The fact it wasn't a mainstream sport back then gave it extra appeal. My life gained fresh meaning and depth as I discovered it was okay to embrace my rebel within.

Learning to climb on gritstone, for me, meant learning to climb with no ropes. Most of the routes were relatively micro in length and it was easy to be tempted to just try the next move and climb that little bit higher. It was technical climbing and relied on good balance, timing and strong fingers. In sweaty conditions, it was impossible to move well, but when the temperature dropped, the friction would increase, and it was game on. I made a vow to my young self that I would only climb solo if I felt I could reverse the moves and climb safely down as well as up the routes.

For years I have been captivated by the all-encompassing intensity of this movement, and the control and concentration it requires from me. Withdrawing from everything but the next move, sensing everything, but thinking nothing. The temperature and texture of the rock, the pressure and angle of my toes, the purity of joy that floods through my system as I pull safely over the top to become one with the view.

What running barefoot through this forest has revealed to me is a similar state to the one I experience while climbing with no ropes. I'm still learning moves and need complete focus to avoid injury, but thankfully the consequences aren't quite so dire if I do get it wrong.

6

THE WINGMAN & THE EIGER

In 2013 life was heading in a good direction. Our two children, Imogen and Jemima, were growing up wild and happy in the Highlands and we felt we were starting to achieve a good work-life balance. Julie had stepped back from TV and set up a small boutique campsite with her sister Sophie on her family's farm, while my TV career had started to take off. The sleeper train provided a long but spectacular commute from Fort William to London. Often, I would rattle myself to sleep as the sun set over Rannoch Moor then wake up in Euston, a bit crumpled but ready for work.

I thought it wise to proceed with caution. I could see how easy it would be to get sucked into this exciting world and end up spending all my time away from home. I didn't really want that. Neither did Julie or the girls. So, if I took on a big job, I would aim to spend the same time, if not longer, back home afterwards. Over the course of five years, I worked myself up from runner/driver to producer/director and was lucky enough to go on some fine adventures in the process.

The highlight so far had been filming a recreation of Sir Ernest Shackleton's extraordinary tale of survival in Antarctica. After his ship *Endurance* was crushed by sea ice in 1921, he and his men had no choice but to set sail in their lifeboats to the wildly remote glaciers of Elephant Island. They survived this treacherous crossing, and for many of the men their upturned boats became makeshift homes on the island, while Shackleton and five others continued their mission. Unbelievably, in their exhausted state, they managed to navigate using the stars, a sextant and plenty of dead reckoning, towards the tiny spec in the vast Southern Ocean called South Georgia. Once on solid ground, the journey wasn't over. They were on the wrong side of the island and had to cross over uncharted glaciers and mountains towards a whaling station in Stromness, where finally they were able to raise the alarm. Remarkably, all Shackleton's men survived to tell the tale. It is one of the greatest survival stories of all time.

It certainly was an epic shoot. The series producer was my friend and colleague Ed Wardle. Strong, wiry and usually quite stoic, he was indeed a man prepared to suffer for his art. Dressed in woollens, armed with nothing but foul-tasting pemmican and a camera, Ed somehow survived squalor, sea sickness and trench foot to capture the whole journey from on board the replica of the lifeboat that Shackleton had used, the *James Caird*. Ed was also a veteran of Everest, having summited three times while filming *Beyond the Limit* for Discovery Channel. As we'd spent so much time together, Ed knew it was my dream to film in the Himalayas. You can only imagine how excited I was when he came to visit me in Fort William to share some big news. Once I'd made coffee and we were settled down with our Hobnobs, Ed revealed all.

Joby Ogwyn, an extreme athlete from Louisiana USA, wanted to make history by becoming the first man to jump off the summit of Everest in a wingsuit. To ramp up the pressure, this attempt would be broadcast live to a global audience on Discovery Channel. I sat transfixed, nearly missing my mouth with my cup, as Ed went on to explain the details. I hoped beyond hope that this preamble was leading in the direction of a job offer.

Joby sounded likeable and laid back, audacious enough to dream this wild dream but grounded enough for it to be taken seriously. First, he would climb to the summit. There he would assess the wind speed and choose one of three special speed-wings (a stripped-back hang glider) that best matched the conditions. He would then change into his wingsuit, take a deep breath, and jump from the summit while attached to this wing. This would hopefully give him enough propulsion away from the slopes and buttresses of the mighty Southwest Face beneath him. Once far enough away from the clutches of the cliffs, he would unclip the two karabiners that held him to the frame of the wing and let rip through the thin air. The precise location of his landing was still to be determined, but he would be flying in the direction of Base Camp where the crew would be waiting for him with high fives and hugs. Ed looked me directly in the eye and I sensed the big question was coming.

'How do you fancy being a high-altitude cameraman, Joe?' I nearly kissed him at this suggestion, but then things got even better. To create a load of hype about the jump, we would have to head out to Switzerland and film his preparations on and around the Eiger. 'Are you free next week?' Was this real? All my adventure dreams had come true over the course of one cup of coffee.

Humans were hurling themselves off cliffs every which way you looked as we entered the Lauterbrunnen Valley, deep in the Swiss Alps. It was one of the few places in Europe where it was legal to BASE* jump and it seemed to be perfectly sculpted for this purpose. High alpine pastures gave way to sheer 1000m limestone cliffs, with exit points for jumpers dotted everywhere. It was

---

* **BASE jumping** (/beɪs/) is the recreational sport of jumping from fixed objects, using a parachute to descend safely to the ground.

particularly busy on the first day of our shoot and we arrived to find a BASE jumping event happening in one of the fields on the valley floor.

Dance music was banging out of the open boot of a Fiat Panda, as lemmings landed one by one close by. I caught the eye of one guy smoking a spliff as he prepared his parachute by the side of the road and received a hazy nod. I smiled back and hoped he was paying close attention to what he was doing. Surely he would want a clear head for such a task?

It was most peculiar to see the sky full of flying humans, but quite a thrill. Unfortunately, one poor soul didn't make it after misjudging their trajectory and landing on some power cables. This cut the power to the whole valley but, judging by the efficiency of the clean-up, it wasn't an uncommon occurrence. Within minutes a helicopter had retrieved the body of the deceased and in less than an hour, it was business as usual. The music started up again and soon the sky was full of flying fabric once more. I was half expecting *Another One Bites the Dust* to be the DJ's opener.

Joby wasn't put off by this in the slightest. We were soon filming him as he prepared his speed-wing high up in this spectacular valley. With tight curls of blond hair, blue eyes and a bulging six pack, Joby looked like a comic book superhero as he put his tight black wingsuit on and got himself psyched up to jump. After much prep, he was ready to take flight. Unfortunately, his first attempt saw him somewhat magnetically drawn towards the roof of the only barn for miles around. We breathed out a collective 'Oh shit!' as we stood by helplessly, but Joby's reactions were quick enough to get him up and out of danger and we all giggled with nervous relief. He jumped, released, and repeated his flights like a man possessed, until he felt confident that his plan would work. The more time I spent with him, the less crazy it all seemed. With meticulous planning and a bit of luck, I started to believe that his wild dream could indeed become an historic reality.

We wanted to leave Switzerland with a sensational sequence and Ed's vision for it was both spectacular and ambitious. We hired two helicopters, one with a Cineflex camera mounted underneath, to follow Joby through the air, and one for us to get into position on the ground. Joby would be flown to various locations around the valley for climbing and running shots, gaining height each time. We would then drop him on the summit of the Eiger and later cut it together as if he had run the whole way up.

In the sequence it would appear as if Joby had then jumped off the summit, but in reality, we would fly him a little higher and he would launch out of the helicopter instead. He would then 'buzz fly' the Mittellegi ridge on the left edge of the mighty North Face. This meant to fly in as close proximity to the ridge as possible, without actually hitting it. The adrenaline rush, I was assured, was out of this world!

I was happy to take his word for it. Ed would direct from the Cineflex chopper and I would follow Joby before, much to my delight, being delivered to the Mittellegi hut halfway up the ridge for the all-important flyby shot. Joby's mate Marshall Miller would jump as well, covered in GoPro mini cams to give us his POV. To keep me safe, I had my old mate Brian Hall joining me and I was mighty pleased to have him there.

Brian had been there and done it all. He was one of the industry's most experienced adventure safety consultants and had overseen action-packed sequences on films such as *Touching the Void* and the James Bond franchise. He was also a legendary climber. I'd first met him during my apprenticeship with Triple Echo Productions while working in the Outer Hebrides at the beginning of my career, and it took a while to win him over. I was filming on a beach one night and struggling to carry everything by myself. I asked Brian if he could help by carrying my tripod. He looked at me with an unreadable expression on his stoic, storm-chiselled face and said, 'No'. I continued to scuttle along the shore with a camera, rucksack and tripod all hanging off me. I resisted the urge to react, but I may have sworn a bit under my breath. He was old school, and I knew he was just testing me. The key was not to crack.

I managed to win him over later in the shoot when a volcano erupted on Iceland and all flights were cancelled from Stornoway airport due to poor air quality. I volunteered to drive him all the way to Glasgow to catch his train and, as a result, drove myself right into his good books where I've stayed ever since. Now here we were, four years later, about to make a fly over the most famous North Face in the world. Even Brian was excited by this prospect. So much so, he even offered to carry my tripod.

An early start meant we were rolling on the ridges of the Silber-horn by sunrise. Joby indeed looked every bit the hero as he climbed and ran along with a salmon pink sky and milky Alps behind him. It looked as if he was running through a Toblerone advert, and I was nearly yodelling with delight. We would shoot for a while then clear frame for Ed's Cineflex to swoop over. Nowadays all this could be done by drone, but we were certainly enjoying the high budget Hollywood approach.

Once we were confident we'd got the first half of our sequence in the bag, both helicopters came back to land outside the Bell View Hotel in Grindlewald and we got out with a swagger. This was the location for the Clint Eastwood classic *The Eiger Sanction* in 1975 and, more importantly, for our breakfast that morning. We waited patiently with our croissant and coffee for the perfect conditions we needed. Swirls of cloud clung to the North Face behind us as we ate. It was touch and go for what seemed like an age. Finally, the radio crackled into life and it was all systems go.

Brian and I jumped in the back of the helicopter, my heart pounding. We were instantly treated to an incredible perspective of the mighty North Face route that I'd read about in Richard Haszko's books at school all those years ago. We could see it all – the Traverse of the Gods, the White Spider, the Exit Ramps – and my tongue was practically stuck to the window.

Our pilot couldn't land at the Mittellegi hut due to lack of space, so just hovered with one skid on the ridge and indicated that we should open the door and jump out. '. . . 'kin brilliant!' Brian muttered as we hit the snow and huddled down over our kit.

Even for him this was obviously a special moment. When the roar of the engine was clear, we uncrumpled ourselves and took it all in. Crisp alpine air hit our lungs and our eyes were filled with the majesty of the mountains. High five Brian, *Yodel lay hee hoo.*

As we sorted ourselves out, our helicopter flew back to pick Joby up and fly him to the summit of the Eiger. This cinematic wide shot we were after was slightly precarious. Our hero would have to waddle a few steps to get into position. In his big wingsuit this wasn't easy, and the summit dropped away steeply on all sides. Ed was also concerned that the down draught from the helicopter's blades might catch his wings and send him spiralling back down the North Face.

To avoid this spectacularly bad outcome, mountain guide Hans Rudi was there to keep him safe with a tight rope. Unfortunately for Hans, he also needed to keep out of shot. As soon as they landed on the summit, Hans got to work burying himself in the snow while setting up an anchor and holding on to Joby's rope simultaneously. It was a big ask certainly at the limit of what was safely achievable, but somehow, we got the shot.

As we waited for the jump, I knew I must contain my excitement as I was in danger of giving myself a headache. Everywhere I looked I could see amazing shots, but I had to keep focused on the main event. It had cost a good few grand to put me here and I knew this was very much the most expensive single shot of my life. I meticulously set up my tripod with a loose head, so I could track them smoothly through the air as they whizzed past and practised the move a few times. 'Any sign of them?' I enquired. Brian was busy scanning the air. 'Nothing yet, Joe. Still looks like they are flying round the top.' We checked the radio: it was definitely on. No need to panic.

As nothing continued to happen for a while, I couldn't resist getting just a few shots as it was one of the most spectacular vistas I'd ever seen. Brian stayed on lookout but was also busy snapping away himself. He was as happy and relaxed as I'd ever seen him as we waited in wonderment for the all-important radio call. They still seemed to be taking a very long time, but I wasn't bothered. This was my best morning at work ever and my first taste of the pressure that I knew I would have to get used to on Everest. That was until Brian shouted, 'Bloody hell, Joe, they've jumped!'

Somehow the radio call hadn't come through and we now had two black dots in the sky hurtling towards us at an alarming rate. Over two hundred kilometres an hour to be precise. My camera was on the tripod facing the other direction. I leapt across the snow and grabbed it off just in time to swing round and catch them full frame as they ripped through the air. They were just metres away, so close I could see the whites of their eyes as they exploded past, whooping as they went their wild way. I saw now what a mess this would be if they got it wrong. I had maximum respect: their mental control was extraordinary. I zoomed in and tried to follow them as they continued their journey down but, without my tripod, my wobbly shot was painful to watch. They'd easily out flown the Cineflex helicopter as well, so the rest would be on Marshall's mini cams. My heart was racing as I switched to review mode to check if I had got the shot. Thank God it was there, as I don't think Ed would have taken me to Everest if it hadn't been. Brian thankfully also filmed a backup on his SLR. Don't tell him this, but his shot may have been better than mine.

The helicopter came for us. We raced down the mountain after Joby, finding him in a meadow at the bottom, safe and sound. His post interview was extraordinary. 'The human body is not designed to fly . . . my brain is making entirely new neural pathways.' Adrenaline was making his eyes bulge and hands shake as he ripped himself out of his wingsuit. 'Are you ready for Everest, Joby?' Ed shouted from behind me. Joby grinned the grin of a wild man and looked straight down the barrel, 'I'm gonna climb Everest, jump from the summit and land at Base Camp. Boom. Boom. Boom.'

7

EVEREST JUMP LIVE

2014

Breakfast time at the Yak and Yeti Hotel in Kathmandu and there was a buzz around the room. Excited gossip murmured from the tables of other expeditions, and everyone seemed interested to know what we were up to. Our table of four also made up our climbing camera team. Joining Ed and me were Matt Green and John Griber, both of whom had summited before. I was feeling slight pangs of imposter syndrome as I sipped my juice and thought about what to eat. I was easily the least experienced, both at altitude and with a camera, but had to keep my game face on and a firm handshake for everyone I met. Of course I knew what I was doing, I just hadn't done it yet. We were being looked after by Alpine Ascents, a well-respected American expedition company who were also responsible for the mammoth logistics involved for the shoot, which easily dwarfed anything I'd been involved with so far.

On the table opposite were Joby and his friend Garrett Madison – an accomplished young mountain guide who had set up Madison Mountaineering that same year. He would be responsible for looking after Joby all the way to the summit. They were the rock and roll stars of the room and had that aura as they tucked into what looked to me like the mega-buffet of dreams. It was truly an international affair: you could have Chinese, Indian, Continental or, as some hungry climbers did, everything in one go. All eyes were on Joby as he ventured up to get himself an extra sausage. 'Look, that's the man who's gonna jump!' I tingled with nerves and excitement myself as I caught his sparkling eyes. I smiled back at him, accidentally putting a dollop of lentil curry on my croissant and carried on as if that was exactly the taste combination I was after.

After two weeks of trekking and the odd bit of filming, we found we weren't quite so popular when we arrived at Everest Base Camp. The broadcast was not only hugely ambitious, but also needed an enormous amount of resources. So much so that an old Russian military helicopter was required to deliver approximately twelve tons of fuel, food and equipment as far as Namche. From there, it was estimated that four hundred yak loads and three hundred porter loads would be needed to carry it all on up to Base Camp. We were in danger of using all the fuel and porters in the Khumbu and this raised a few eyebrows among the other expeditions we were sharing Base Camp with. We ended up having a human and yak train running continuously for a week or so, as Peli after Peli case containing all the kit arrived and a castle wall was built with them around our camp.

The huge generators required to power the whole shebang didn't make our stay any less inconspicuous either. Neither did the two gigantic satellite dishes we needed. Many regulars on the mountain were questioning our presence and objective. Was this a brave and heroic attempt or a just reckless TV stunt? Certainly everyone at Base Camp had an opinion and we were the talk of this temporary canvas town.

As a climber, I was feeling this conflict myself. I'd grown up among those who had served apprenticeships climbing in

Scotland and the Alps before they felt ready to head off to the high Himalayas. Once they had gained the right amount of experience, they could then plan expeditions to these mighty peaks with a greater understanding of the environment they were entering. There were no helicopters or internet or gourmet food on offer, but this is precisely why they went. Venturing into these new realms meant leaving the modern world behind to experience a much simpler existence, knowing that they had the skills to get out of trouble if things went wrong.

This was a different thing altogether. If Everest was a circus, we were the main act. We had well and truly brought the pressures and pollution of the modern world with us and perhaps the scale of our project was highlighting just how commercial Everest had now become. Was this in fact the new normal? It was my first taste of commercial mountaineering and a fascinating position to find myself in. It was camping like I'd never camped before, and it was hard not to love the luxury. Before each meal, a steaming hot towel would be presented to us so that we could clean up before tucking in. We would then be treated to freshly prepared sushi with a cold beer, or perhaps steak and chips washed down with a cup of French red. When I picked my camera up to film Dave MacLeod just a few years ago, I couldn't have dreamed that it would lead me here. I felt for the climbers who were complaining, but hey, they'd chosen to come to Everest. There were plenty of other quieter peaks out there after all. Regardless of all the debate, I was there to do a job and was loving being a part of something so huge and exciting. That was when I wasn't thinking too deeply about what lay ahead.

NBC had teamed up with Discovery Channel for the shoot and had sent a tremendously talented crew of technicians, producers and riggers from New York to make it all happen. Judging by how they were running around at the beginning though, they were obviously more used to setting up for the Olympics than problem solving at high altitude. At 5,364m above sea level, just eating a sandwich at Base Camp was a struggle for the first week or so, let alone figuring out how to put on the most ambitious live broadcast ever. With only around half the oxygen than there was at sea level, slow and steady was the only way. It took the crew a while to find this out, but once they had got into a sustainable rhythm, they worked wonders to get our outside broadcast unit up and running.

This meant we were able to talk to HQ in New York by landline via a satellite in space. A remarkable effort in a short time, the only problem being it was now constantly ringing with requests. One of the many potential problems for the production was the fact that it was impossible to predict exactly when we could go live. The approaching monsoon from the Bay of Bengal wasn't concerned about the pressures of TV scheduling or stressed-out producers. The mighty storm clouds would arrive when they arrived and that was that. Season over.

Historically, there was a period of more stable weather during the month of May, when the summit wasn't being smashed by the usual storm force winds. This short window gave by far the best chance of a successful summit, and it was hoped that we would go live at some point on the 11th or 12th May, which statistically had proved good days in the past. One problem with having such a tight window was that potentially hundreds of others would be going for it at the same time and there was no way we could control that. Things could get interesting up there.

When we were eventually to go live, all four of us cameramen would be in constant communication with the New York office via a headpiece. They would direct us as to where they wanted our cameras pointed and which size shots to give them. Our signal would beam down to a dish at Base Camp, out to space, back to New York, then out to our worldwide audience. There would be a slight delay of a few minutes, just in case something went horribly wrong.

It was sensibly decided that Ed, Griber and Matt would follow Joby to the summit, with one of them stopping at the South Summit to give us a different angle of shot. As I was the least experienced member, this made sense, though the summit could still be a possibility for me if one of them got ill. There were two suggestions for me. One position would be at around 8,000m on the Lhotse Face with a very long lens. The other was between Camps 1 and 2 in case he decided, or was forced, to land there instead of Base Camp. Either way, I was set for a great adventure and was spurred on by the enthusiasm of my guide for the trip.

He came in the shape of Andy Tyson, fresh from the Teton mountains of Wyoming. 'You must be Joe,' he had greeted me in the lobby of the Yak and Yeti a couple of weeks earlier. My attempted firm handshake was met with a relaxed high five that immediately put me at ease. He was wearing a funky patterned trekking shirt and shorts, and his smart baseball cap had floppy wings of curly brown hair poking out the sides. We were surrounded by piles of kit that had just cleared customs and were scratching our heads, trying to make sense of it all.

'I'm Andy. I think we're in for some fun times, dude!'

When not guiding, Andy was writing, exploring and creating innovative ecological power solutions for a greener world, with the company he co-founded, Creative Energies. He had designed the solar panel power system that Alpine Ascents were using at Base Camp, a system they still use today. As he was obviously a man of high talent, I was lucky that he had come out of his office to take this gig. He was my roommate for the trek in and a constant stream of positivity. I loved his humble nature and attitude towards life, as did the many Sherpa friends that he had made on previous trips to the Khumbu.

One evening during the walk in, we sneaked off to climb on some incredible looking boulders we'd spotted just outside Lobuche camp. Bonded by this shared passion, we set a load of new problems and climbed harder and harder until I fell off. 'You don't want to twist your ankle now, mate,' Andy wisely warned after watching me wobble and slide down a crack with cold fingers. Thankfully he was spotting me, and his intervention prevented too much of a bump.

Out on these boulders, I trusted my new friend enough to confess that I did feel a little anxious about my lack of high-altitude camera experience. I'd only ever been to 6000m before and was spending increasing amounts of time secretly sweating in my sleeping bag about the task at hand. Ed had fought hard to get me on the team, and I really didn't want to let him down. I also didn't want to burden him with any extra worry. The pressure I would be under shooting live to a global audience from 8,000 metres, tracking a pea-sized Joby travelling at two hundred kilometres an hour, wearing gloves, googles and an oxygen mask while taking direction from New York, was a bit more than I was used to. As was the lens I was given to use for the job. It was longer than my forearm. I had tried to look impressed as it came out of the case, but actually I was petrified. What if it all froze up? What would I do then?

I was playing with the big boys and needed to find my big boy pants. Luckily Andy lent me the perfect pair, woven out of his calm optimism and tremendous experience. He boosted me with a great pep talk that evening and from then on, we became a team within the team.

~

On the 18th April we were due to start our acclimatisation by climbing to Camp 2 and back down again. The importance of acclimatising slowly at altitude is well known. You must give your body enough time to create extra red blood cells to help combat the lack of oxygen in the thin air and in your blood. Acute Mountain Sickness (AMS) is very common if you try to go too high too quickly and needs to be taken seriously. If it is not dealt with, AMS can rapidly develop into life threatening pulmonary or cerebral oedema.

It was planned that I would film this first foray onto the mountain, following our Sherpa for behind-the-scenes footage to run alongside the main event. We were blessed to have one of the world's nicest men in charge of our Sherpa team, the legendary Sirdar, Lakpa Rita. He had summited Everest seventeen times, but you would never know, such was his humble and modest nature. In the year 2000, Alpine Ascents sponsored him to move to Seattle and become a full mountain guide. He was one of the first Sherpa to start working internationally like this and you may recognise his handsome face and warm, infectious smile from the labels of Sherpa clothing company.

It was a good job he had so much experience as he would certainly need it. On this first trip alone, he had to organise twenty-seven Sherpa to carry our loads, which had pretty much emptied his home village of Thame of all its men. One of those men was fifty-six-year-old Camp 2 cook, Ang Tshering. He had recently finished building a new guest house in Thame and, after twenty seasons of cooking up high, this would be his last journey to Camp 2, before retiring to run his new business.

We wanted plenty of Sherpa stories to be included as part of the production and I thought Ang Tshering's story would be a great one. It was planned that we would make a couple of rotations up to Camp 2 and Camp 3, before heading down and resting at Base Camp before the final push. This meant making multiple journeys through the longest and most dangerous mile on planet earth: the Khumbu Icefall.

Guarding the upper slopes of the mountain from Base Camp, this enormous tumbling glacier grinds down in perpetual motion from Camp 1 towards Base Camp by about three feet a day. Crunching ice cliffs into collapse and ripping open bottomless crevasses as it goes, it is considered by many to be the most dangerous section of the whole Everest climb. As there is no alternative route from the south, the only option is to take a deep breath, say a few prayers and go for it.

Once inside, you can hear the grind and groan and there's nothing to do but move quickly. But even this doesn't make it any safer, as you may well be rushing towards a block that's just about to collapse. As if this is not enough, the gigantic walls that flank either side of the Icefall are loaded with hanging seracs (huge ice blocks) ready to blow their colossal load at any moment. It would be a completely ridiculous proposition on any other mountain and a feature like this would usually be avoided at all costs. But this is Everest and things are a little different. It is considered a risk worth taking as, once you are through it, the route above becomes more straightforward. If you are strong and lucky enough, the summit is then yours for the taking.

A team of climbing Sherpa known as the Icefall Doctors scout the best way through each year. They use cheap nylon ropes to lash aluminium ladders together over the many gaping crevasses and up ice towers that can sometimes be four or five ladders high. This effectively opens the mountain for business. Above the Icefall another team of climbing Sherpa take over the fixing of the mountain and secure the slopes with ropes that lead all the way to the summit. Once these are in position, climbers can then clip in and follow them all the way. The route through the Icefall changes each year dependent on the condition and configuration of the endless jumbles of teetering ice towers and crevasses inside. This year the chosen route pushed left, which gave the most straightforward way through, but consequently strayed further into the range of the huge seracs hanging heavy off the slopes above.

8

DEADLIEST DAY

On 17th April, the day before we were due to start our first rounds of acclimatisation, the whole team gathered for our Buddhist Puja ceremony. Ancient mantras were chanted through thick juniper smoke to appease Miyolangsama, the goddess who dwells at the summit of Sagarmatha (Everest) and evoke her blessings for safe passage.

Each of us brought one piece of our climbing equipment to be blessed with good luck at the Puja Altar, which had colourful prayer flags spidering out from it to the four corners of our camp. I took a photo of Julie, Imogen and Jemima and my ice axe. We were right beneath the Icefall, which provided a stunning but intimidating backdrop to our emotional ceremony. In just a few hours I would be in among it all and I was both excited and petrified by the thought.

A thin red chord was tied round our necks for strength and protection and rice was blessed and thrown three times to ward off danger and any evil spirits who may be lurking. We were encouraged to take some of this magic rice and use it on the mountain if need be. I loved this wild suggestion and made sure there was plenty in my pockets. Our Sherpa team didn't hold back from the booze and were guzzling the local Raksi brew by the gallon. Fair play to the thirsty bunch I thought, but I did wonder how they would be feeling when we left at

2am the next morning. I hoped they'd already packed their bags.

We shared the responsibility of filming among the four of us, so we each got the chance to participate. The heady mix of strong booze and thin air certainly added to the mystical nature of the ceremony. It climaxed with a strange shuffling dance with all the expedition arm in arm staggering forwards and backwards together as one unified team. Barley flour erupted into the air and was smeared on our faces for one last dose of good luck. With our pockets full of magic rice and the ceremony over, we now felt ready for anything. Almost.

I left the ceremony with a slight headache to have a lie down and prepare my bag for the early start the next morning. Having a camera kit to sort out as well as all my personal stuff meant that meticulous planning of how to pack was required. I didn't feel meticulous, I felt a bit sick. Instead of any packing, I passed out in a hot haze for an hour or so then woke up with an even worse headache than I'd started with. My hammering heartbeat was synchronised with the throb in my head and dots appeared if I closed my eyes. I fumbled around for a few sweaty minutes, trying to make some progress, but it wasn't happening. All I could do was bail out and head to the dining tent to rehydrate.

Ben Jones, our lead guide, happened to be outside and was pleased to bump into me. 'There's been a change of plan,' he told me, in his usual warm and friendly manner. 'I think it's best we let the Sherpa team get ahead and set up before we join them, so you're not going anywhere in the morning, dude.' Music to my ears. 'Good call!' I agreed, before dosing myself with ibuprofen, swallowing as much water as possible and staggering back to doze in the late afternoon sun.

~

At 2am my feverish sleep was interrupted by a startling dream. I awoke to find myself shouting *Grandma* out loud, while my hand clutched at the air outside my sleeping bag. Vivid dreams at altitude are very common and can often be quite psychedelic. This one was so spookily intense it took me a few seconds to be released from its grip. My grandmother, Joan French, who had passed away a couple of years before, was reaching towards me with outstretched arms. Just before we were able to join hands, I had woken up shouting her name. This had never happened before and though it felt incredible to sense her so close and real, I was unsettled by the vividness with which she had appeared. I wondered if the other guys had heard me shout? Outside, I could hear the tinkling of metal and smelled wafts of juniper as our twenty-seven Sherpa prepared themselves for their journey. I buried myself deep into my down nest, feeling another pang of relief that I wasn't going anywhere, and dozed off to the sound of crampons crunched off into the distance.

I woke with a start at 6.45am. This time reality was even stranger than my dream. Morning had broken with a supersonic boom from the direction of the Icefall and its reverberations were still bouncing off the steep mountain walls all around. I poked my head out of the tent and saw Ed running towards me. 'Camera ready – quick, Joe,' he barked. 'I'm heading to the helipad, you cover things here.' Adrenalin started to surge as I realised what the explosion must have been. Pulling on any clothes I could find, I burst out of my tent with my camera rolling.

It was instantly and devastatingly apparent that we were dealing with a tragedy of mammoth proportions. A gigantic ice block, later estimated to weigh around 64,000 tonnes, had calved off the western shoulder of Everest then fallen approximately 1,300ft before detonating with nuclear force about one third of the way up the Icefall. Exactly where this year's route went. Everything in its path must surely have been obliterated. The mix of ice and rock and debris exploded then re-exploded until the whole width of the Icefall was covered by a ghostly plume.

Mountain guides Michael Horst, Ben Jones and Andy Tyson were already out there when I found them with my camera. 'We're gonna need all the shovels this camp has,' Michael shouted, pulling his rucksack on as he marched past. Ben was crouched down, sorting his crampons out. 'It's gonna take us a couple of hours to get up there,' he said. 'None of us have been up there yet and we're not acclimatised.' Lakpa Rita had heard over his radio that at least five of our Sherpa were unaccounted for and had already left. We were all fearing the worst.

I headed to the Alpine Ascents communication tent where Joe Kluberton, our Base Camp Manager, was somehow managing the already constant stream of radio traffic.

'Can you confirm if any of the Sherpa were wearing avalanche transceivers?' came a request crackling over the airways as I found my frame. It wasn't common practice for Sherpa, guides or climbers from any expedition to be wearing them. They couldn't help anyone survive the initial blast, but could be helpful now to pinpoint a body's location. With a deep sigh, Joe double checked with Michael who was now stomping through the Icefall. As he suspected, it was a negative.

'No transceivers, I repeat *no* transceivers.'

Although he was enormously upset, Joe's composure was remarkable. He was doing an amazing job holding it together and making sense of the minute-by-minute updates that were flooding in. The whole of Base Camp had simultaneously become one team, with all expeditions unified by the awful events unfolding. It was hard to get a handle on exactly how many men had been killed or injured, but it was obvious to everyone that the death toll was high. 'We've got the first helicopter with a longline arriving in thirty minutes,' Joe relayed to the helipad crew, whom Ed was no doubt filming. Reports of some survivors started to come through, but agonisingly, there was still no news about our missing men.

Filming such a tragedy as it unfolded was a difficult thing to do. I was aware of the extra pressure my camera could be putting on Joe. He seemed all right with my being there, but I kept myself as inconspicuous as I could. The camera helped as it felt like a barrier between me and the tragic reality of the situation, at least to begin with. I kept my mind occupied by thinking of shots and the sequence but, as we waited for updates on our missing Sherpa, it was becoming impossible to keep my emotions at bay. I'd never cried while filming before, but it was hard to focus the camera at times because of the tears. I would film for a while then go outside to cry, then come back in before starting the whole process again.

Gradually the sequence of events became clear to us. We learnt that the huge serac had smashed into the Icefall near a level section called the Football Field. The first group of Sherpa moving through that morning had come to a difficult area where multiple ladders were needed to climb the ice towers and cross the large crevasses there. One of the ladders had been damaged by falling ice, so they stopped to fix it. This caused a tailback for a hundred or so Sherpa who had to wait patiently to get moving again. I was haunted by the thought of them all hanging out there and chatting, unaware that these were their last moments. I was also very aware that if there had not been a last minute change of plan, I would no doubt have been there filming as they fixed the ladder.

Lakpa Rita took just ninety minutes to race up to Ground Zero and was faced with a horrific scene. Legs of friends sticking out of the snow, bodies entombed in ice, half-buried men, some conscious and some not. The highest concentration of casualties was found in a mass grave where eleven men clipped to the same line had taken a direct hit. They revealed themselves one by one as Lakpa and his colleagues pulled them out. Only Dawa Tashi, who had ended up on top of them all, survived.

Despite the danger of another avalanche being very real, and the consequences laid out before them, brave rescuers continued to arrive and did what they could among the blood-stained ice. Andy Tyson climbed one of the ladders to investigate the leg sticking up out of the snow and found it was that of Dorjee Khatri, Garrett Madison's Sirdar. His leg was badly fractured, and his body heat had melted the snow around him, before refreezing and encasing him in ice. Andy, Garrett, and Ben Jones began the process of carefully chipping around Dorjee's body with the picks of their axes to try and excavate him, as much needed help from the helicopters started to arrive.

Soon rescuers were being flown up while dead bodies were being flown down. By this time, it was mainly a recovery mission. The stiff contorted corpses of our friends began to rise from the Icefall on longlines beneath the helicopters to hang like pendulums, between two worlds. Battered bodies soared through the sky in blood-soaked bags, each one drawing Base Camp to a standstill as we collectively looked up and tried to take in what we were seeing. This horrific process went on and on as the bodies came down one by one. Dorjee's body wasn't one of them. He remained in the ice that night as, despite their best efforts, Andy and the others had run out of time and further work would be needed to free Dorjee from his icy grave.

The final death toll was sixteen. All of them were Sherpa, including the five from Alpine Ascents: Ang Tshering Sherpa, Nima Sherpa, Tenzing Chottar Sherpa, Mingma Nuru Sherpa and Dorji

Sherpa. It was the worst single tragedy to ever occur on the slopes of Everest and Base Camp was awash with grief. Men we had drunk and danced with at our Puja less than twenty-four hours before, were now dead. The kind eyes of our Camp 2 cook Ang Tshering closed forever before his retirement dream could be reached. Husbands and fathers and brothers had been lost, many from the same village of Thame.

The days after the tragedy were dark and difficult as the process began of reuniting the bodies of the deceased with their grieving families. In all, twenty-eight children were now fatherless and the grief at Base Camp was starting to merge with anger. For many Sherpa, the idea of carrying on with the season was out of the question. They needed to be home in their devastated communities and needed time to grieve for their friends and brothers.

Not everyone felt the same. Base Camp remained busy with western climbers who had paid thousands of pounds to get there and many were waiting for things to calm down so that they could carry on. This caused a huge amount of tension between the climbers and the Sherpa and among the Sherpa themselves. Many simply couldn't afford to miss a season's wages and were prepared to climb despite pressure from other Sherpa groups to call the whole season off. All this raw emotion and confusion was not helped when the Nepali Government offered the families of the deceased just £400 on top of their insurance pay-out in compensation for their loss. This was taken as a huge insult and fuelled the fire further. Days of meetings and indecision ensued, so we kept a low profile as the atmosphere became more volatile.

For us cameramen the decision was clear. There was no way we would even entertain the idea of carrying on. Our team had been blown apart and all of us were deeply upset and emotionally exhausted. Three bodies were still encased in the ice and the thought of climbing over them to carry on was simply out of the question. As our leader, Ed Wardle was a brilliant spokesman for us. His blunt Scottish realism was exactly what we needed and the argument he presented for us to cancel the jump was clear. The bosses at Discovery and NBC supported our position, though it seemed that, for a short time at least, Joby was still keen to jump.

I'd eventually managed to call Julie on the day of the disaster, but it took some time. News of the tragedy had spread around the globe instantly and while she was waiting anxiously to hear that I was okay, I was still covering the events as they unfolded. It must have been an agonising wait for her. When I spoke to her again the following day, with the good news that I expected to be home soon, I got an awful shock.

Julie had just read on Joby's Facebook that '. . . today is a brighter day and we are staying on the mountain to honour our friends and complete our project.' I was dumbfounded. How could he be thinking that this was the right thing to do? It wasn't just Julie who had read this statement, but the rest of Base Camp and the outside world. As you can imagine it hadn't gone down too well. In fact, Joby's post had poured petrol onto a smouldering fire and as the smoke rose, he soon realised his error of judgement, took the post down and got himself out of there quick.

Here it may be relevant to mention an event that took place the previous year that involved the late Ueli Steck, Simone Moro and Jonathon Griffith. The Lhotse Face was being fixed between Camp 2 and Camp 3 by a team of Sherpa who had reportedly put out a request that no one was to climb until the job was complete. Either the trio of Europeans hadn't heard this request or chose to ignore it and climbed past the affronted Sherpa, disrupting their progress in the process.

A heated argument broke out on the slopes and insults were exchanged before both teams retreated to Camp 2 to sort things out. What ensued was both alarming and frightening. A high-altitude brawl broke out as a large mob of vexed Sherpa made their way to the climbers' camp to demand an apology for both ignoring their requests and for the use of some offensive language towards them. Violence erupted. Punches and kicks were thrown, with Ueli taking a serious blow to the head. Despite retreating to his tent for safety, rocks were hurled at him and one of them pierced straight through the fabric. Apparently, it took an intervention from independent climber Melissa Arnot and IMG expedition leader Greg Vernovage to calm the situation down before it got completely out of control.

What this event revealed was the tension and resentment that had been growing among some of the climbing Sherpa community towards the way that the lucrative Everest industry was being run and how they were being treated and represented within it. They were shouldering the most risk while being paid the least, and the traditional working relationship between the Sherpa and their western employers was being openly questioned. A new generation of qualified Sherpa guides wanted more control of the mountain themselves and a bigger slice of the multi-million-dollar industry it had become.

This feeling was not shared by the whole Sherpa community. For many of them, the western companies had been loyal and respectful employers. They brought in much needed finance and development to the area and showed a level of care for their employees that went far beyond their responsibility for them on the slopes. I'm summarising what was in fact a highly complex situation. Needless to say, with all the grief, anger and confusion at Base Camp, Joby's Facebook post certainly had the potential to incite a similar reaction from some of the Sherpa community as that which Ueli and his team had provoked the year before.

For the first time I felt uncomfortable at Base Camp and kept my camera well hidden, wishing for it all to be over. All eyes were on us and, at certain camps, warm smiles turned to cold stares. Eventually after days of debate, meetings, grief and anger, the 2014 climbing season on Everest was declared over by the Government of Nepal. For the first time in history, the slopes of Mt Everest were closed for business. We were all finally, and thankfully, told to go home.

Our American colleagues from NBC stayed behind to film extra footage for the *Everest Avalanche Tragedy* documentary that our project evolved into, while we went and got very drunk in Kathmandu. Joby was at the bar in the Yak and Yeti, and I was pleased to see him and be able to say goodbye.

I liked him and felt privileged to get a glimpse into his high-octane world. His unfortunate posting on Facebook wasn't intended to upset anyone, it was just a misjudgement in the heat of the moment which he obviously regretted now. He vowed to return and give it another go, but was still upset with Ed. On the evening of the day of the avalanche, a live broadcast for Channel 4 News has been set up. Ed had sensibly declared to the world that the season was probably over, but Joby didn't feel that this was Ed's call to make. This was his project after all. Many years of preparation had been spent and with an incredibly expensive live broadcast all set up it was obviously difficult for him to let it all go.

We tried to let it go that night, but no amount of Gurkha beer could shift our collective sadness. When we eventually made it to the airport a couple of days later, there was a simple wooden coffin lying on the floor next to our bags with a name scribbled on it. As we moved towards the check-in desk, I watched in silence as it was slowly shunted across the floor.

9

STRENGTH

'I'm going to dig a fire pit,' I declared, over a cup of tea in our back garden. Julie was perched on a grassy bank with Jemima snuffling at her breast. I remembered Edie Irwin's advice about getting my hands in the soil, so digging a big hole seemed like a good idea. The expedition had ended so abruptly. I was home with my family but tormented with thoughts of children whose fathers never returned. The colourful prayer flags I'd stretched out between the trees served as a reminder of both my blessing and my sadness. As did the thin red cord round my neck. I didn't even know if the Sherpa who had tied it was still alive.

'It's a great idea my love, but perhaps you want a proper spade?' As usual, Julie was right. I put my trowel down and went to the shed to look for one. She flashed a grin at me as I walked past, reminding me of our first date.

I had been excitedly waiting by the window of my house in Fort William. Julie was selling a camera, and I was interested in it. Really though, it was just an excuse to see her. She was a surfing, tree-loving TV producer who had worked for Comic Relief and the BBC. I was seriously impressed.

So far, there was little sign of her. I was starting to wonder if I'd been stood up. Finally, my phone rang, 'Hey Joe, I'm so sorry. I'm in a bit of a predicament!' I put my shoes on and went out to investigate. What kind of predicament?

A little way down the hill, I found out. After realising she had driven up the wrong driveway, Julie had reversed back out. Unfortunately, a low brick wall got in the way. Her mate's Nissan Micra was now hanging precariously over it. As I approached, she was grinning, clearly amused, if not a bit embarrassed. 'I nearly bailed out and called home for help,' she confessed, 'but something made me call you instead.' I think I fell in love with her there and then.

A couple of Polish chaps appeared, chuckling at our problem. 'You need help?' they asked. 'Yes please!' With a bit of sleeve rolling and grunting, they lifted the back wheels up and pivoted the car back onto the driveway. 'No problem!' They laughed and went on their way, with an extra swagger to their steps. And so began the story of Julie and Joe.

'That's more like it!' Julie said, as I returned with a bigger spade and got to work. The freshly exposed soil had a smell of earthy goodness, and the rhythm of digging felt comforting and familiar. I could relax into it. That afternoon I began the process of stripping the garden of all its gorse. Pulling out deep, knotted roots felt satisfying and therapeutic.

As the sun set, our fire was lit. We sat together and watched smoke and flames dance and crackle, roasting our marshmallows in a glow of orange and pink. I thought of funeral pyres in Nepal and how blessed I was to have my family around me. Imogen was three and Jemima six months. Flames flickered across Julie's face as we sat and enjoyed our marshmallows, all of us oblivious to the monster lurking in the shadows.

'I don't want to worry you but . . .' Julie began.

It was now late September. I was in Vancouver, about to fly home after six weeks filming. A letter had arrived, reminding Julie to go in for a cervical smear test. While having coffee with friends, she confessed she might not bother. 'You have to go!' her friend Carrie insisted. What wise advice that turned out to be. The test results were back and worryingly abnormal. She needed to go into hospital for follow up checks '. . . but please don't worry about anything my love, I'm sure it will all be okay.'

Don't worry? I paced around the aeroplane all the way across the Atlantic. Thankfully I was home by the time Julie went for her follow-up appointment. It was immediately clear to the doctor that she had cervical cancer. To what extent it had spread was unknown so far, but samples were taken and all we could do was wait and worry.

The monster lurking in the shadows had moved into our house, but we didn't know how big or scary it was. Internally our lives had been turned upside down, but externally everything was the same. Julie looked healthy and our girls played on. Our future was being held hostage by these results. Until they came, we weren't sure what we were dealing with or how to deal with it. Then one morning, I heard Julie speaking on the phone. From the tone of her voice, I could tell she was speaking to a doctor.

I took Imogen and Jemima out for a walk in the woods. Imogen was absorbed in her own make-believe world. She became a lost princess known to us as China Paradise who needed help finding her way home and being kept safe from wolves of the forest. Jemima, who was now just nine months, snuggled into my chest as we played. Imogen's imagination was the best place we could possibly be. We arrived at the beech tree next to the river, where a small burn flows into a bubbly pool. I heard a car door close on the other side and looked up to see Julie approaching. She looked hunched and pale. 'Mummy, Mummy we've found our fairy den, come and see!'

'Mum's a bit busy now, sweetheart.' Julie shouted above the suddenly deafening roar of the river. 'They want to see me in person,' she told me. Her words seemed to punch me in the stomach. I sank down, unable to move.

'What's wrong with Mummy?' Imogen asked, sensing the change in us.

'Nothing at all, darling,' I whispered. 'Have you seen any fairies yet?'

As Julie drove off to find out exactly how ill she was, I pulled myself up and chased Imogen back through the trees and home to cook supper. Was that wolves in the distance? Quick everyone, run! I turned the TV on for the girls, while scrabbling around the kitchen, trying to find enough composure to cook sausages. What could the doctor be telling her? Why could he not tell her over the phone?

'Can we watch Topsy and Tim? When's food ready?' My hands were shaking as I squeezed ketchup onto Imogen's plate 'Where's Mummy? What's for pudding?'

By the time Topsy and Tim had finished, I'd gone through just about every imaginable scenario. I heard the car crunch over our gravel. My stomach was hollow and I was conscious of a pulse throbbing in my neck. Julie looked even paler when she walked in, but it wasn't until we got the girls to bed that we could finally speak.

'I have stage two cervical cancer,' Julie said. 'It has spread out of my cervix, so a hysterectomy won't work.' I held my head in my hands for a moment, as if hiding behind them would make it all go away. Julie was calm as she went on to explain our new reality, already full of determination. I was trying to hide my tears.

A team of expert doctors had met to discuss her treatment plan and, as she was young and fit, they thought a five-week intensive course of chemotherapy combined with radiotherapy was the best way forward. She would have chemo once a week and a blast of radiotherapy every day. Then, as a daunting grand finale, she would receive four rounds of precise internal radiotherapy, otherwise known as brachytherapy.

'The doctors think that if I can cope with treatment, I've a good chance of full recovery,' Julie explained. There was already no doubt in her mind that she would get through this.

'Yeah, babe, it's all going to be fine.' I reassured her. Silence hit the room as we hugged. For a moment there was nothing else to say. Julie broke away and started to potter around the kitchen. 'Now,' she continued, 'I'm just gonna make a loaf of bread.'

By late October, Julie's treatment had started. This meant a daily round trip of one hundred and fifty miles to Raigmore Hospital in Inverness, and a lot of organisation and help was required. Jemima wasn't too pleased about losing her place at Julie's breast. A plastic bottle of formula milk served by her dad wasn't quite the same.

Our families were incredibly supportive and we all shared the responsibility of childcare and driving. The community around Fort William also gave us masses of love and support. We would often return to find pre-cooked meals on our doorstep and offers of help looking after Imogen and Jemima. One friend even arranged for a thorough deep clean of our house while we were on the road, which boosted our spirits no end.

To begin with, the treatments didn't seem to be affecting Julie too much, but after a couple of weeks of chemo, the many bends of the A82 between Fort William and Inverness became an awful daily ordeal. Julie already suffered car sickness at the best of times. Now she had radioactive juice in her veins to calibrate round the corners as well. It was so rough on her, but true to form she gave no hint of any self-pity. This almost became frustrating.

Surely she needed a good moan or worry or cry or something? I certainly felt like it at times.

During her first chemo session we had tried to have a laugh, playing a rather silly game of guess the ailment round the ward, while I massaged her feet. By week three though, the side effects of the treatment were noticeable. A hotel in Inverness was the only solution. Each day we were humbled by the care and dedication of the hospital staff and Macmillan nurses, who made sure that we were always looked after. This wasn't the first time we'd relied on the NHS for life saving treatment. Both Imogen and Jemima had been delivered by emergency Caesarean section. Imogen had been a full ten weeks premature. Without the NHS I wouldn't have a family at all.

As the treatments progressed, the toll it was taking on Julie became more obvious. She lost a lot of muscle and was weak and nauseous most of the time. The chemo was killing cancer cells, but also killing her healthy cells as well. She was being stripped back to the core of her being, revealing just how strong she was.

We tried to keep things as normal as we could around our girls. I think they were the main reason Julie stayed so strong. Thankfully they were too young to be aware of what was going on. Maintaining routines of parenthood was important for Julie, but also tough to watch. I would tell her to rest, but it was no good. I would still find her back in the kitchen, her frail, shaky hands kneading dough, insisting on baking bread for us every time she came home, even though she couldn't eat it herself.

I had to work hard to stay grounded and avoid feeling – and being – negative. I gave up drinking alcohol, so I was fresh for the girls every morning and we would dance to happy tunes to start the day. *One Love* by Bob Marley was a favourite, as was Xavier Rudd's *Follow the Sun*.

If I could exercise for just an hour a day, I felt much better. Julie's calm acceptance of our situation was an inspiration, but also a bit maddening. She still hadn't grumbled about anything, so how could I? Was everything really that okay? I was worried and afraid but didn't share this with Julie. Instead, I rode my bike up into the mountains and found views big enough to distract my attention, for a while at least.

My number one spot became Intake Ten, just below the rising pyramid of Carn Mor Dearg. I could cycle up there to get my mountain fix and still be back home within an hour. The intake itself hides just out of view and is a place of powerful vibration. Vast torrents of water are captured here and diverted through an underground network of pipes and tunnels to the aluminium factory miles below. A ten foot square grate protects this powerful intake to prevent debris falling in. I found by chance that this was the most exhilarating place for yoga moves.

I could stretch myself out into downward dog right on top of a thirty foot waterfall, hypnotised by its all-consuming rumble and rage. When the sun came out after a heavy downpour, the back draft in the tunnel would push a fine mist out of the grate, leaving my body surrounded by thousands of tiny rainbows. I imagined this mist to be cleansing and recharging me. After praying to any god that might be listening and a quick dip in the icy pool, I returned home, ready to be strong again.

By December, the finishing line was coming into view. The chemo and radiotherapy treatments had finished, and Julie had a short break before the treatment she was fearing most – brachytherapy.

The low December sun was setting behind us as we drove quietly to Aberdeen. 'Normal life is gonna seem so easy after all this,' Julie joked, but she was right. We would certainly not be taking so much for granted. What had been revealed to us was the knife-edge we had been blindly walking along while wrapped up in our everyday worries, stresses and aspirations. What did any of them matter without good health?

Laura Marling's *Blackberry Stone* played on our stereo as we pulled into the hospital car park. We sat for a moment and let the song finish before getting out. Julie was as physically weak as I'd ever seen her, almost skeletal. I could have picked her up and carried her in with one hand. And now it was time for her toughest challenge yet.

In hospital she would be padded out with cotton wool. A radioactive rod would be inserted inside her. As she remained completely still, the rod would be plugged in and she would receive a short blast of radiation, exactly where the tumour was. This would happen twice. A week later the process would be repeated, then her treatment would be over.

'I hope the doctor has a good aim,' Julie whispered as she entered the pre-op room, strapped down to her trolley. Her ability to find humour in the most adverse of situations was staggering. I held her hand as she stared at the ceiling, unable to move any muscle in her body so as not to disrupt the very precise positioning of the rods.

With a kiss on her forehead, it was time for me to leave. I went outside to the car park and cried, while Julie closed her eyes and settled somewhere deep within. Later she explained how the only way to deal with it all was moment to moment. Resistance to the process was futile. All she could do was accept each moment and, if she could cope with that one, she could move on and cope with the next. Her whole life was condensed to a series of breaths.

10

RUNNING MAN 3: SUPER NATURE

2020

The crumbled wall forms a border between the trees. Native on one side and planation on the other. It is a busy place. If I do whack my foot or get poked by a branch, I stop. In my fizzy stillness, other worlds come into view. This one belongs to the tree dwellers.

Tits and finches fill the air, darting from birch to birch above my head. Long-tail, great, coal and blue can usually be spotted, alongside their friends – chaffinch, greenfinch and, if I'm lucky, a bullfinch. Red squirrels watch from high branches, weaving grass nests with tiny claws while greater spotted woodpeckers headbutt their way to wiggly treats.

Inside the spruce, I rarely find a feather. Occasionally I disturb a woodcock. It leaves its ground-nest vertically, before shooting off through the trees like an X-wing fighter. But with barren pickings at ground level, its busier up in the canopy, where the spruce tips can be found. Pine martens use these tracks, but I don't think live among these trees. I often spot the scat they leave as they sneak through, on stealth missions to eat our chickens.

Badgers do live here. They have different setts throughout the forest, burrowed deep into banks and used in rotation. I once discovered the full skeleton of a roe deer at the entrance to one, its miniature grooved antlers still attached to its skull. Whether an opportune find or a skilful hunt, the clan of badgers had a big drag on their claws that night.

At the end of the wall, a long winding coniferous corridor can be found. It is lined with a thick carpet of bone-dry pine needles which give the ground extra crunch beneath my feet. I'm enticed into a full sprint. Cambered corners and sculpted ramps provide perfect take-off and landing pads between giant fingers of spruce thrusting deep into the ground. Here I must be fully present. With an increase of speed comes an increase of risk. I'm playing the knife game with my feet, quick stepping through a stretching moment of time, just avoiding this branch or that root, eyes fixed on my next step. Motion tears start to build under the strain of my stare but I dare not blink them away until I have passed the foot jabbers. Instead, I keep my eyes wide, waiting for an opportunity for one big strong blink to clear the water and sharpen the blur. An injury-free passage through the forest is a team effort between my conscious and subconscious self. My body is their puppet but there are no strings attached.

Rounding a rising corner, I pop out next to a sparkling burn lined with luminous green mosses. Within its sepia waters are shimmering flakes of quartz, magnified bright by a liquid lens lapping over pink pebbles of moraine. There is no way to run barefoot here as it's too boggy, so I squelch across slowly, feeling my feet slide into the mossy gloop beneath.

A rotten birch tree has fallen across the track. Its soft mushroomy funk tickles my nose. Polypore fungi hover like mini spacecraft over its trunk, busy breaking it back down into the earth from which it came. It's thrilling to think of the subterranean messaging going on around my toes. Whether warning each other of danger or helping sick relatives by sending extra nutrients, the trees are in communication. I want to tune in.

It's become my custom to pause here for a while, as my heart settles down after that explosion of pace, plugged into the earth, tingling with endorphins, feeling grateful that I'm able to run here at all.

During my thirties, running was impossible because of the unbearable knee pain it caused. An MRI scan confirmed that a torn meniscus disc was the problem. This tough cartilage acts as a shock absorber between one's shins and thigh bone and is quite a handy substance to keep intact. I had a medial tear and was given the choice of whether to have an operation to remove the damaged area or just to leave it be. I chose the latter.

Years of climbing and carrying a heavy camera on one shoulder hasn't helped my posture. I'm often out of line. Even before the medial tear, running always exaggerated my misalignments and caused me pain. Perhaps this was because I wasn't running consciously, or thinking about how my feet were landing, where my weight was, if I was heel striking or not. Perhaps the shoes themselves were also interfering with my natural foot strike, causing my muscles to compensate, exaggerating the problems further. I wanted to run, but it would always leave me feeling beaten. I became frustrated that at such an early age, I was being limited by my injuries.

Then I discovered barefoot. If we are born to run, our bodies must have evolved to do so without compensating for how our running shoes effect our stride. In the same way as a bird shouldn't injure a wing through flying, we shouldn't injure ourselves through running. Could it be that my shoes and technique were causing the problems, rather than my body itself?

Now that my feet have toughened up to splinters (which took a year or so and an Avon foot spa most evenings), I can run pain free day after day on the soft, springy trails in the woods. The earth absorbs the impact of my strides down into itself rather than sending shock waves back up my shins and into my joints. The terrain also forces my core muscles into conscious action. They need to be engaged to maintain my equilibrium as I leap across ditches and duck between trees. I never realised just how important they were. But now, whether running through a forest, along the flat or up a mountain, my core muscles are central to all movements. As a result, my lower back and legs have never felt stronger.

The forest has taught me how to run again. I no longer suffer knee pain, my calf muscles have stretched, my foot arches have risen, and my soles are as tough as leather. This anatomical transformation has taken a few years and is ongoing. My feet soon soften if they spend too much time in shoes. I can't say for certain that going barefoot is the only reason, but wherever and whenever I run now, I feel like I'm running on solid foundations. In shoes or not, my torn meniscus causes no problem at all.

11

CITY IN THE SKY

2015

'It's about the unsung heroes of Everest . . .' Lou Dew enthused. She was behind her desk at Raw TV in Shoreditch, London. I was walking next to Neptune's Staircase in Banavie. Early March sunlight bounced off the canal and Imogen's little finger curled round mine. '. . . you know, the characters behind the scenes, making the summit possible, but whose stories are often overlooked.' As Lou went on to explain the details, I felt myself smile. 'We would be flying out in March and would love to have you on board if you're interested?'

Only three months had passed since Julie's final treatment. My initial reaction was to say no. Surely, I shouldn't be heading halfway round the world after everything we had just been through. Should I? Try as I might, I couldn't stop thinking about it. I loved the premise and could see what an enthralling series it could make.

Every March, the barren Khumbu glacier transforms into a bright and busy canvas town. Housing rich and poor, with their dreams, disasters and rivalries, it caters for all needs with its bakeries, clinics and shrines. At the peak of the climbing season, it can be home to upwards of one thousand people from all around the globe. In our film, Sherpa, guides, doctors, porters

and pilots would be the stars of our show, not the climbers themselves. This would turn the usual format on its head and, after the
heroics I'd witnessed the previous year, it felt like a series that
needed to be made. It was also a precious chance to see all those
I'd said goodbye to in such horrible circumstances the previous
year. 'I think you should go,' Julie said straight away. This was
typical of her. Whether through stubborn will-power or spiritual
wisdom, she still hadn't grumbled about her ordeal once.
Although still recovering, she was feeling strong and, with her
parents close by, wouldn't be short of help if she needed it. It
wouldn't be a dangerous trip, as I wouldn't have to climb anything: a couple of weeks of meetings in Kathmandu, followed by
a trek to Base Camp.

'I'm in!' I told Lou the following day, and that was that. Soon I
was splitting my working week between London and the Highlands again, enjoying curry with the hipsters of Hackney by night
and waking up with deer over Rannoch Moor in the morning.
The sleeper train between Fort William and London must provide one of the world's finest commutes.

Because of tension around film crews at some parts of Base
Camp, this was to be a stealth mission. Many a camera operator
had previously got themselves into trouble by sticking their
camera where it wasn't wanted. I'd certainly felt uncomfortable
at times the previous year. The annual residents could spot a producer in pursuit of a sensationalist storyline a mile off. This
wasn't what we intended. Our goal was to gain access for a positive, celebratory series, but TV being TV, there would still need
to be enough jeopardy and drama to keep the audience engaged.
The key to this was to gain trust and, as a climber myself, I took
this prerequisite very seriously.

Our team of three consisted of Lou Dew as line producer, Sam
Maynard as executive producer and me as development producer/

cameraman. We would shoot everything on a small, discreet camera to keep it low-key. Sam would fly out to join us for the trek to Base Camp, after Lou and I had got things underway in Kathmandu.

This was my sixth trip to Nepal. I was excited as we touched down, but the familiar smell of Tribhuvan International Airport conjured sad memories in an instant. Thoughts of the Icefall and Julie chased round my head as we waited for our bags. Now I was here, I was wondering whether I should have come back at all.

Outside, the streets were marvellously manic. Chapati wallahs on dusty street corners, monkeys running riot on roof tops and brightly coloured trucks spluttering though mud, with Shiva portrayed on their sides. Lou was experiencing this sensory bombardment for the first time and her presence helped to dispel my sense of doubt. It was fun to see her eyes dart from scene to scene as she took it all in. 'Wild place!'

The taxi arrived at the familiar gates of the Yak and Yeti Hotel. I'd never have been able to afford to stay here as a backpacker and loved this new normal. My room was huge, with fine views over the well-manicured gardens and Nepali art on the walls. Come the morning, I felt positive and bounced down the stairs, back to the breakfast buffet of dreams, heading straight for the fresh mango juice. Lou was already at our table with her laptop, notepad and coffee and we were both happy as we began our work.

I was really enjoying being with Lou, who was obviously brilliant at spotting a good storyline as well as looking after all the logistics, finances and everything else. She was a strong sports climber, more used to clipping bolts in the sunshine than climbing at altitude. She had travelled extensively though South America and been up high in both Bolivia and Peru, so knew well what to expect. Lou had been working on this production long before I had become involved and researched just about everyone and everything at Base Camp. As we looked though her extensive notes, we felt like detectives searching for leads to follow, towards all those great stories we knew were out there waiting to be told.

After a tasty breakfast of fruit salad followed by stuffed parantha and pickle, I disappeared up to my room to start my enquires. In the lobby I bumped into Garrett Madison. 'Hey man, great to see you,' he said. I could see my scruffy reflection in his cool shades. It was great to see him too, though his presence stirred another pang of sadness. Last time we spoke had been just after the tragedy, behind the cooks' tent, trying to figure out what to do. Standing next to him, grinning sweetly, was his girlfriend and expedition doctor, Marisa Eve Girawong, known as Eve. They were glowing with health and looked more like a couple of young athletes heading to the Olympics, than mountaineers heading off to Base Camp. 'How would you like to come up to Camp 2 with us?' Garrett offered after I told him what I was doing there. 'You what? That would be amazing, dude!' I wasn't quite sure what the Raw TV office or Julie would have to say about it, but in that moment, it didn't matter. Whether I climbed or not, Garrett's simple offer had made me feel very welcome.

The perfect man to kick start my enquiries was undoubtably my new friend Andy Tyson. He seemed to know everyone who was anyone on the Everest scene and I trusted his judgement completely. We had a long chat that morning and he was delighted to be involved, hinting that he could perhaps be available for the shoot the following year if it was to go ahead.

Andy and his wife Molly had just returned from Nepal, where they were volunteering as instructors at the Khumbu Climbing School. Set up as part of the Alex Lowe Charitable Foundation, the school's mission was 'to increase the safety margin of Nepali climbers and high-altitude workers by encouraging responsible climbing practices in a supportive and community-based pro-gramme.' It was a brilliant organisation and when I was cc'd into an email with Vice President Conrad Anker and Dr Steve Mock later that morning, I felt we were up and running in the right direction. I must also admit that Conrad was a hero of mine.

I'd read about and watched many of Conrad's adventures. One in particular had stayed with me. During an expedition in 1999, it was Conrad who found George Mallory's body high on the North Face of Everest. After identifying Mallory's opaque corpse, face down, frozen in time and rags of tweed, he needed to alert the rest of his team to his discovery. The problem was that he didn't want to draw too much attention to it over the radio waves, so Conrad was cryptic and careful with his words, when he delivered the classic line, 'Last time I tried to climb a boulder problem in hobnail boots . . . I fell off!'

Andy and I went on to talk about Julie's illness and the tough time we'd had since I'd last seen him. I told him about Garrett's offer of a trip to Camp 2 and wondered what he thought of the opportunity. 'Life is for living,' he enthused, 'but if it's likely to cause significant angst back home, maybe reconsider?'

Making the decision to return to Nepal was relatively easy, especially with Julie's encouragement, but what extra stress a trip to Camp 2 could generate at home was unknown. Julie still had lots of healing ahead of her. Ever since waving goodbye, I'd been questioning my decision to leave. It was helpful to reveal this inner conflict to Andy and I was grateful for his balanced response. This needed some serious thought. Perhaps the best idea was to forget about climbing and just stick to Base Camp. At least then I would be safe from danger.

12

RETURN OF THE IMPOSTER

Before we began trekking to Base Camp, there was plenty to do in Kathmandu. First stop was back to the airport to meet with Captain Siddhartha Gurung at Simrik Helicopters. He was Executive Director of the company and one of the brave pilots who had been involved with the longline recovery mission the previous year.

As cool and composed as the Buddha himself, his matter-of-fact stories about high-altitude helicopter rescues were staggering. 'We sometimes take the doors off if we go really high,' he explained. 'This means we can really push the machines to the limit.' As we looked round one of their B3e helicopters, we learned that it was this model that once landed one skid on the summit of Everest and had been used during the record 7,800m longline from the Lhotse Face. These achievements both involved a different helicopter company but highlighted just how incredible the world of high-altitude flying was.

As this was just an initial meet and greet, I'd not planned to do any filming. Instead I had arranged to go back in a couple of days and film a little then. Then just as we were about to leave, a call came in. 'There's been a report of missing climbers high on Annapurna,' Siddhartha explained, as he put on his helmet. A team came from nowhere to prepare the helicopter for flight. Lou and I looked at each other. Brilliant! I thought and whipped my camera out. The perfect start to our sizzle.

My excitement soon turned to frustration. Regrettably I'd not yet spent any time learning the ways of this unfamiliar camera. Because it was small and compact, I had wrongly assumed it would be easy to use. As the sweat started to prickle on my forehead, I was quickly learning that this wasn't the case. The focal ring also doubled as the iris ring, so you needed to switch between the two, which was proving quite tricky in the heat of the moment. In hindsight, I should have just switched to full auto mode and played it safe. But I didn't, so ended up shooting the whole sequence either slightly out of focus or under exposed. It looked more like an amateur wedding video than a sensational sizzle.

'You all right, Joe?' Lou enquired, noticing my change in mood as we taxied back to the hotel. 'Think my footage is a bit soft,' I confessed, feeling I could trust her enough to be honest. The experience had left me feeling like an imposter again, one who couldn't even use a camera. 'You'll be exposed as a fraud,' a silent voice warned me. I looked out of the window. 'It will be fine, mate,' Lou reassured, as if she could hear my thoughts.

There was something else though. Somewhere on Annapurna, real people were in real trouble. Did I really think that was brilliant? Whose voice had that been?

The first time I had experienced imposter syndrome was a decade before. I was twenty-five and had just moved to Fort William to take a job with the rebellious arts project, Room 13.

Its founder, Rob Fairley, looked like a cross between Socrates and a Yeti when I visited Caol Primary School to see what the project was all about. He bounded barefoot around the studio, wearing green paint-splattered overalls, in heavy philosophical debate with his eleven-year-old boss and management committee. 'What age can you start being an artist?' was the question. Thoughtful kids gave interesting answers to this as they feasted on Chomps and Space Raiders. Behind him, a curly haired girl was lost in a world of elephants, painting one after another on a huge canvas, or at least it looked huge because of her size. Others were playing chess and sketching, as Bach's Symphony in D major played quietly in the background.

The pupils ran the studio as a business. This had enormous educational and developmental benefits. My job was to start a similar studio in nearby Lochaber High School. The problem was, I wasn't an artist.

I tried pretending but was soon exposed. I had a 6ft square canvas that I invited my first group of students to stick interesting bits of nature on. I was hoping it would somehow create a coherent collage. It didn't. It started to rot and smell and ended up being a half-finished health hazard. I had to think of something else. Music. I had worked as a DJ in Sheffield under the name French Toast and played guitar in an indie band. Rather than an art studio, perhaps it could be a recording studio?

I began strumming in my empty room, a poster of Bob Marley on the wall, waiting day after day for students to arrive. They would poke their heads round the door at lunch time and ask, 'Who are you?' It was a good question. I had experience as a classroom assistant, but that was it. I wasn't part of the teaching or support staff. I wasn't a member of a union. I had no qualifications. I was a bloke in a school with a guitar and a stool.

In the staffroom I felt uncomfortable, sensing that many teachers were wondering exactly what I was doing there. So was I. Others were more encouraging. They could see the benefits a Room 13 could bring to the high school. I just had to keep believing in it.

The pressure I felt was enormous, though most of it was self-generated. My sleep was affected. Night after night I would lay worrying, listening to the same voice of doubt. Then, each morning, I would head back in on my mission to enthuse sceptical students with the belief that we could turn this class-room into a recording studio. It was exhausting but we eventually did it. I met the students on their level, more like a friend or facilitator than a teacher. I loved this freedom, especially once we'd started making music and films, but it also left me feeling vulnerable, given the lack of available support. I was making it up as I went along, and everybody knew it.

We ended up recording two experimental albums, producing a three-minute wonder documentary for Channel 4 and it helped Room 13 become a global charity. I'd even set a studio up at the HCMC orphanage here in Kathmandu. It was an incredible period of mutual learning for me and the students but had left me emotionally rinsed. I'd taught myself how to film on a PD150 camera in that classroom and ultimately that's what brought me here. Sweating in this taxi with Lou working for Discovery Channel, but still feeling like a fraud.

13

THE BOULDER OF LIFE

It was all happening in Lukla the day we arrived. Our Executive Producer, Sam Maynard, jumped out of the helicopter with his usual zest, snapping pictures and writing notes all at the same time. 'This is incredible!' he exclaimed as we collectively tried to make sense of all the colour, noise and altitude.

Our guide for the trip, Chhongba Sherpa, was smiling as he stood next to our luggage in his bright orange jacket and wide-brimmed hat. I couldn't help but notice the deep scar across his left cheek. Once the helicopter had reloaded and cleared for Kathmandu, he revelled in telling us the reason for the carnival atmosphere. 'Three Lama brothers from the monastery are coming, it's a very special day here.' Monks had travelled and gathered from all over the region to be in their presence. Lukla was awash with maroon robes, yellow hats and loud blasts from long Tibetan horns. 'These brothers are very special,' Chhongba continued. 'They have been reborn as the same brothers seven times in a row.' Sam let his camera swing round his neck and pushed his glasses back up his nose. 'You what? Seven times? What are the chances of that!'

We learnt this remarkable feat was only possible as they were skilfully able to navigate the Bardo Thola (the space Buddhists believe we enter between life and rebirth), to choose their next incarnation. These three brothers were conscious pilots of the afterlife and the excitement and anticipation towards their imminent arrival was palpable.

Intricate symbols of sand were poured by young monks around the front garden of the monastery and the air was thick with incense as the mystical trio came into land. They were greeted by hypnotic drums and loud Tibetan horns as they climbed out of their helicopter. They seemed delighted by their lively reception and smiled and waved before disappearing into the monastery for, I guess, a nice cup of tea. All this evoked a feeling of pilgrimage in me. I was smiling broadly as the familiar trail dropped steeply out of Lukla and our trek began.

The first days felt more like a holiday with friends than hard work. As we wanted to maintain a low-key presence during our mission, the camera stayed in the bag and instead we concentrated on making friends, acclimatising and brainstorming ideas that would give structure to our series.

As we huddled up in a cosy new tea house every night, time with Chhongba was always a treat. 'This is from a fight with a bear,' he told us one night, as we guzzled down our dal bhat. He ran his finger down the scar on his left cheek and it was hard to tell if he was joking or not. Every word he spoke was delivered with a warm smile. It turned out later that this was a true story.

By happy coincidence, he was also director of Nepalese operations for the Khumbu Climbing School and was delighted that we'd already been in contact with Conrad and Steve. Along the tea house trail everybody recognised Chhongba in his bright orange jacket. He was treated like Khumbu royalty, but was always humble, with his kind and gentle nature. One thing he rightly kept emphasising was the need to go slow and not to do too much.

Sam was managing the enforced change of gear well, though I think it was in his DNA to be going at full pelt. His workload had been cleared by Raw TV so he could focus solely on this project, but given the chance, he'd be off on a mission to get reception on his phone. It was obviously proving difficult for him not to want to stay across the other projects that were on his desk, however far away he was. He'd been my Exec on the Shackleton expedition, so I was used to his high energy and liked him a lot. As we followed the roar of the Dudh Koshi river towards Namche Bazar I enjoyed hearing of his past. He had been a pioneer of the lifestyle I had been living in Fort William – live local, work global.

At the dawn of the eighties Sam had moved to the Isle of Lewis to work as a photographer for the Stornoway Gazette. There, he spotted an opportunity. At that time, the press in London had no choice but to send a photographer if they wanted to include a photo in a news article. Not any more. Sam invested in a scanner and started wiring his photos to various London newsrooms, which changed the game for them completely. He didn't stop there. To promote the Island's art and culture to the world, and to invite the world to Lewis, Sam was part of the team that founded An Lannntair, Stornoway's first art gallery. It opened in 1985 and is still going strong now.

After a decade spent building an award-winning TV and Internet company, Sam hatched plans to create a large glass clamshell on a beach in Lewis. One end would be a thriving studio space and creative hub, while the other would gradually shrink down to become a tunnel housing a high-speed optical cable all the way back to the mainland. The idea that he could be working within an international community, while being able to nip out for a quick surf between meetings, was inspired. This project was never realised, but perhaps he was just too far ahead of his time.

~

After a week or so, we got to Pheriche, a gathering of small-holdings and tea houses at 4240m, just a couple of days' walk from Base Camp. Sam and Lou were both looking a bit ropy as they sat in the shadows of our empty tea house, choosing food from a menu they had no appetite for. I didn't feel great either. The familiar throb in my head had come back if I moved too quickly. There are no short cuts when it comes to acclimatisation. You've got to give your body time to produce the extra red blood cells that it needs to carry more oxygen around your system. Simple as that. The best way to do this is to climb high, sleep low and rest often. Even that doesn't guarantee success and some folks find they just never really acclimatise.

Before we retired to our rooms, I checked my emails. Andy Tyson's wife Molly Loomis had been in touch. She was a writer and had a deep understanding of the place, having written extensively about Everest ER, a medical outpost at Base Camp, which we hoped would be part of our show. She had also worked as an instructor with the Khumbu Climbing School, and it felt like a dream team could be coming together. I emailed both Molly and Andy before bed, boosted by their support. We were closing in on their friends at Base Camp and I was looking forward to meeting them.

It was a short distance to Lobuche, the next village, but a 700m gain in altitude – enough to push many a trekker into AMS (Acute Mountain Sickness). The lodges have a Wild West feel to them, complete with a questionable water source and a reputation as a place where folk regularly get ill. I was feeling better after my rest day, so left Sam and Lou with Chhongba and got myself ahead to shoot some scenic shots.

En route, you must climb over the Thokla pass and cross the haunted plateau beyond. Under the swoosh and sway of a thousand prayer flags, you are reminded of just what's at stake as you venture ever higher. Stretching out in all directions are countless memorial and Mani stones, dedicated to climbers and trekkers who never returned. I'd interviewed Joby beside one the previous year and asked him about the consequences if things went wrong. It was hard to comprehend that just a couple of weeks later, sixteen men would be dead, all of whom were working to make the mountain more comfortable and safer for us. My upset and sadness had been overlaid by the trauma of Julie's illness, but the closer I got to Base Camp, the more these emotions seemed to be resurfacing.

This year I was grateful not to have the pressure of having to construct a sequence there. I was free to explore and contemplate the emotional charge of the place and the invisible force that Everest seems to exude. I set my camera up for a time-lapse and lapsed off for some time myself. I lay down behind Scott Fischer's Mani stone and allowed my thoughts to drift and mingle with the colourful prayer flags, fluttering and muttering away in the infinite vastness of deep blue space above.

I thought about Andy Tyson during that dreamy hour, about the boulders just ahead of us that we had climbed the previous year, before everything had gone so wrong. I pictured them in my mind and tried to remember the subtle sequences required to complete each problem. With eyes closed I could feel my fingertips curl over cool granite lips and see the crystals I was gambling with as my feet scampered briefly upon them. At the top of one block, when I confided to Andy that I was secretly struggling with self-doubt and imposturous feelings, he gave me one of the best pep talks I'd ever had. It came back to me in my semi-slumber.

Andy metamorphosed the boulder we were sitting on to become an actual metaphor for how we can grow into ourselves through overcoming challenges. 'After all, unless we challenge ourselves in life we go nowhere.' I nodded in agreement. 'First you must choose a boulder problem that is appropriate to you, like the one we've just climbed. Too easy and there's no challenge, too hard and there's no real chance of success.'

Broom-sweeps of small avalanches expanded out over cliffs behind his fluffy hair and his eyes were clear and sparkling with his truth. 'The key to finding that success,' he continued, 'is finding the perfect line that challenges you enough to feel a sense of accomplishment. One that is possible only through commitment, focus and self-belief.' He paused, and his helpful words hung in the thin air. The 6000m summit of Lobuche East loomed over us. I traced a line in my mind's eye to the top. 'The battle with your own fear and perceived limitation is one you can win over and over again. That's the beauty of bouldering! But you must remember the first step . . . choosing the appropriate challenge to you.'

I remember being unconvinced that climbing to 8000m for the first time and shooting live to a global audience was an appropriate challenge to set myself, but Andy's words and wisdom gave me a huge boost. If this was a very large boulder problem, we would climb it together and with double the self-belief we couldn't help but succeed. We clambered down the boulder and tried a harder line as the sun set. I fell off and we called it a day.

As I left the Mani stones and trekked on, I compiled a plan for my afternoon at Lobuche to distract my weary legs and the first signs of a slight headache returning. First, I would rest, drink a few gallons of tea and eat two peanut butter chapatis and a Mars bar. Then, I would see if Andy had responded to my mail before heading out to our boulders to repeat our climbs of the previous year. I was sure he'd like to see some photos of them at his desk in Wyoming.

I clattered though the door of our lodge and was immediately hit by a heavy wave of distress in the room. Eric Murphy, a guide from Alpine Ascents, was in tears in the corner, surrounded by his clients. I must have been dozing for longer than I thought, as Lou and Sam had both arrived and were sitting close by with their heads down. Lou looked up at me with sad eyes as I came in.

'You may want to sit down, Joe. There's been some terrible news.'

I was informed that Andy Tyson had been killed that day when the small plane he was in got into difficulties and crashed shortly after take-off. He had been with two of his colleagues from Creative Energies. All four people on board lost their lives.

It was almost a year to the day that I had shared a room with Andy here in this same lodge. I couldn't bear it. After sitting with Lou and Sam for a while, I staggered outside into white silence and cried and walked and cried. With heavy steps I trudged to our boulder and sat beneath, allowing gentle flakes of snow to accumulate on my down jacket and hat until I was covered. When I found some composure, I shook myself down, scuffed the snow off my boots and tried to climb our same line. My movements were stiff and uncoordinated, it was impossible. My tears merged with the snow.

14

THREE TWO ONE

It was a dark night in Lobuche. When I eventually came back to the guest house, Sam was not well. Really not well. We were roommates and he was already in his sleeping bag showing signs of altitude sickness. His oxygen SATs were low, and he had a banging headache and stomach problems. I knew we were in for a rough night. I climbed into my bag in tears. Sam was in the bed next to me, offering words of condolence between his groans of discomfort. We spoke that night about life, death, and the universe until we eventually dozed off into fitful sleep. At some point during the night, I was woken by a wet, ripping noise and my nostrils starting to sting.

'Joe, can you help me, I'm stuck.'

I grabbed my head-torch. Poor Sam was wrestling with his sleeping bag, trying desperately to open the zip that had bitten into the side fabric and got stuck. I got involved in the fumble and eventually worked it free. Sam popped out of his bag and waddled off down the corridor clutching at his buttocks, though judging by the smell and sight, it looked as if he was already too late.

Sam continued to deteriorate. By the light of morning, it was clear the safest option was a helicopter evacuation. He then had to endure a further twenty-four hours of suffering, as thick cloud had rolled up the valley and no flights were possible. For Lou and me, it was a sad farewell to this fine man and friend. His wisdom and energy would be missed, but we had to remain positive. With Lou's steady head and tremendous TV experience, I felt confident that we would still be all right. She had adjusted better to the altitude since Pheriche and, after all her research and preparation, was excited about reaching Base Camp, only half a day's walk away.

I was lost in thought as I dawdled on my own past Gorak Shep. When I eventually arrived at the small cluster of Adventure Consultants' tents, right in the heart of Everest Base Camp, I was greeted by a familiar Northern Irish accent.

'Hello, Joe French!' came from the corner of the dim dining tent as I peeked in. It was Rob Smith.

His tall wiry body emerged from the shadows, and I shook his spade-like hand. When I'd sold my house in Fort William to embark on this new life, it had been Rob's (ex) girlfriend Miriam who had bought it. I remembered showing them round and being delighted to sell it to such nice folk.

Rob was working as a guide for Adventure Consultants, our hosts at Base Camp. He was a modest man of tremendous ability (at the time of writing this, he has summited Everest seven times and K2 twice) and I felt mighty grateful to have a friend there to talk to. The turmoil and grief of the previous twenty-four hours had left me spinning. Add in the altitude of 5364m and I was feeling quite strange.

Word of Andy's passing had spread quickly, and Rob was deeply upset at the news. He had worked with Andy and Molly at ANI Adventure Network in Antarctica, so knew first-hand what a legend he was. With so many people at Base Camp wanting to pay their respects, there was already talk of a Puja ceremony for him. I would try to film it for Molly and his family, and Rob and I would chat with the other expeditions to find a suitable time for everyone to meet.

~

Lou didn't look too well when she arrived later that afternoon. She was pale and breathless, but this was common for most upon arrival. After gingerly pushing a sandwich round her plate and taking a couple of sips of tea, she retired to her tent. Before I went for a rest myself, I said hello to the other expedition members and Adventure Consultants staff.

There was a great atmosphere to the place, which came from the top down. Base Camp Manager, Anthea Fisher, was buzzing about, making sure all was well. Her brown hair was pushed back by white rimmed sunglasses, and she was snuggled cosily into her maroon scarf and bright blue jacket.

'Welcome, Joe,' she greeted me in her friendly way. Adventure Consultants were based in Wanaka, South Island, and a first-rate outfit to be staying with. Anthea was getting to grips with her role as Base Camp Manager for the first time and immediately made me feel at home, as did AC owner Guy Cotter and his partner Suze Kelly, who were also there.

After a blur of introductions, I retired to my tent. Chhongba was happily catching up with his mates and Lou was already out for the count. The summit of Everest was glowing in the late afternoon sun, as I snuggled down to the sound of yak bells and murmuring chat. Despite the usual headache, I felt physically okay. My head was spinning in sad circles though: Andy's smiling face imprinted on my mind's eye; the Icefall looming behind my tent.

Sometime in the night, I tuned into a strange sound. At first, I thought it was the weird way the wind was catching the strings of my tent, until it persisted into an audible whimper.

'Joe, I'm not feeling so good.' It was Lou in the tent next door. I was suddenly wide awake and concerned, as her voice sounded very weak indeed.

I discovered that she had become very sick, very quickly. 'I'll get help,' I reassured her and crunched off through the dark to wake Chhongba and the expedition doctor, David Fitzgerald. With the help of Dendi Sherpa, the camp cook, we carried her by torch light to our media tent. The level of oxygen in her blood was dangerously low. She didn't have a cough or a headache but had suddenly become alarmingly weak and nauseous. Rob Smith and the others had been stirred by the commotion and soon the tent was full. It was quickly decided that the best option was to put Lou in a Gamow Altitude Bag for the night to stabilise her condition.

This bag was pumped full of air, to create a pressure vacuum inside. The purpose of this is to trick the body into thinking it's at a lower altitude and, with the help of supplementary oxygen, this can make the difference between life and death. It was not a long-term solution, though, and if Lou didn't improve when she came out, her only option was to descend. Inside it was sweaty, claustrophobic and frightening. We did our best to keep her spirits up, but her scared eyes through the clouded Perspex window said it all. The bag is functional but labour intensive. Once at a lower altitude inside, it needs regular pumping to keep the pressure stable. Dr Dave spent the night monitoring Lou, while we all took it in turns to do a pumping shift. The kind Sherpa team that assembled ended up doing most.

Back in my tent I didn't sleep much. I just lay with a headache and dry mouth, without the energy to get back out of my sleeping bag and do anything about it. This latest crisis had left me reeling. I must have dozed off eventually as I stirred to hear concerned voices outside my tent. 'Her SATs are dropping right off again, she's not very well.' They had got Lou out of the bag, but despite initial improvements, her oxygen levels plummeted. It was becoming clear that the only option was to call for another helicopter evacuation. I felt so sorry for her. She'd followed Chhongba's instructions to take it slow to the letter and been so careful and determined during the walk in. I knew how disappointed she would be with this outcome, as was I. Right from our first phone call we'd been in this together, sharing excitement and ideas. In such a short space of time everything had gone so wrong.

Hidden behind a mask, clutching her O2 bottle, Lou was carried to the helipad on Dendi's back. Our ears pricked at the welcome sound of approaching blades and we hugged as she disappeared into a bundle on the back seat. Chhongba put his arm round me. 'Think you need some tea, Mr Joe,' he offered in his usual cheerful way. He was right. 'Just the two of us now,' I muttered and followed him back to our tents.

I didn't quite know what to make of my new predicament. It certainly looked a lot different to the one we had started with. After all the tragedy and death of the previous year, I was very sensitive to how the mood would be at Base Camp. I certainly didn't want to upset anyone by filming where I wasn't wanted and become the focus of bad feelings with no one to share them with. I was a climber after all. These were my people. But I was acutely aware that without Sam or Lou the whole production was now on my shoulders. It was my powers of inquiry, judgement and persuasion that would ultimately get this off the ground or not.

Much to my gratitude, Sandra Shuttleworth and Rebecca North at the Raw TV office did their best to defuse as much stress from the situation as they possibly could. Their message of 'Just do what you can, Joe', was welcome, but it was hard not to feel stressed. I love to collaborate and bounce ideas around. Now all the ideas were bouncing round my head with nowhere to go. I thought of Andy Tyson's wise words on the boulders again and gained strength from them. If everything was easy after all, there'd be no opportunity for growth.

Our media tent emphasised my loneliness. It was now unnecessarily large for me, my laptop, hard drive and small camera. This was far from the thriving hub of meetings, inspirations and progress I had pictured. Thankfully, a positive atmosphere around the camp was the norm and, as it happens, another friendly cameraman was based with Adventure Consultants, Scotty Simper. It felt good to have him pop in from time to time, as I tried to figure out what to do next.

Scotty had been employed by a wealthy client to film his journey to the summit. This client also had a private guide and stills photographer, Charlie Mace, to ensure not a moment would be missed. And, to top it all off, every ache and pain was dealt with by his personal physiotherapist, Vicky Hill. She was from Scotland but now living in New Zealand. Despite the altitude, Vicky, with her straw blonde hair, always seemed to be glowing with good health. Her warm smile and lively presence at camp was undoubtedly a positive influence on us all.

After discovering how inflexible the average mountaineer was, Vicky had an idea. Every morning, my empty media tent became home to what must have been the world's highest Pilates classes. There was lots of groaning and grunts, but it was well worth it – despite the headache it tended to bring on. Vicky was even kind enough to give me an acupuncture treatment for my bad lower back, such were her skills. This was luxury climbing with all the trimmings. Very different to the stories of penniless climbers I had grown up with.

One advantage I had as a producer up there was that I wasn't a complete unknown. As well as the bonds I had made the previous year, I also had a family connection with a few characters at Base Camp who knew of my stepfather Andrew Greig from his writings and expeditions with Scottish climber Mal Duff.

~

It is fair to say that Andrew changed the course of my life when he got together with my mum when I was just eighteen. After two failed marriages and a lot of emotional upheaval for my two younger brothers and me, we were delighted the day Andrew's knackered old blue Ford Escort pulled up outside our house on Walton Road, Sheffield. I held my breath as he appeared and uncrumpled himself after his long journey south from Scotland. The first things I noticed were his leather jacket and earring. The earring caught the sun as he stretched. He glanced up at our window with a smile, just as my younger brothers and I ducked away, pretending not to be there. As I peeked back out, this groovy and mysterious man glided over to the boot and pulled out a guitar and a bottle of wine. Get in! I thought, Mum's dating one of those rebel climbers and he even plays the guitar. Oh, happy days.

Andrew had come to Sheffield to do a reading at the Board-man Tasker Award Ceremony with his new book, *Electric Brae*, and because things had been going well with my mum, was staying at our house. He was a poet, novelist and free spirit who could capture a moment in words like a magician. I sat in awe in the audience at the Boardman Tasker, listening to him perform his songs, poems and prose. I had to resist the urge to stand up and announce to the audience that he was dating my mum. Here was a man who was making a living through living his dreams. Something clicked. Now I'd seen it was possible, I knew I stood a chance. Could I get to the Himalayas or even Everest for an adventure and be paid to do so?

It's relevant to mention the event that led Andrew towards the Himalayas in the first place, as our stories are now entwined. In the mid-eighties, a charismatic climber called Mal Duff changed the course of Andrew's life when he burst through the door of his South Queensferry home with a crazy plan. Inspired by Andrew's early book of climbing poetry, *Men on Ice*, Mal wanted to have him come along on one of his Himalayan expeditions to write the all-important book. 'It's there if you want it!' were the words left reverberating round Andrew's head when Mal left that night.

It was a big ask, for Andrew was a complete novice whose skill thus far lay in imagining what it was like to be a climber from his armchair, not tying into the sharp end of the rope. Their mission was to attempt the second ascent of the Mustang Tower – a wild 7276m rock spire in the Karakoram. Like myself as I chased Joby up the Khumbu, Andrew spent a lot of time daunted by the challenge. In the end, the peak was climbed successfully, no one died and Andrew's book, *Summit Fever,* hasn't been out of print since.

Mal's next expedition was a big one: Everest from the Tibetan side. His team, made up of both climbers and clients, would attempt the mighty unclimbed Northeast Ridge. This was the route that Pete Boardman and Joe Tasker, two of the UK's most talented climbers, had gone missing on during a previous attempt with Chris Bonington.

It was to be a huge undertaking both financially and logistically and Mal scaled up to embrace all things commercial. Pilkington Glass were on board as a major sponsor, the team had a media schedule and were making appearances on Blue Peter and the News. Even Kurt Diemberger, the legendary Austrian climber and film maker, came along with his beloved Rolleiflex camera. This was Everest the large way and a big shift from the lightweight Alpine Style approach that so many climbers historically favoured. They didn't make the summit, but no one died, and Andrew succeeded in producing another classic, *Kingdoms of Experience.*

Both books had been nominated for the Boardman Tasker Award previously, but the chair of the judges, W.H. Murray had not been entirely won over. He had not liked Andrew's use of a swear word at the end of *Summit Fever* and the description of a monk picking his nose in *Kingdoms of Experience*. Bill Murray wrote a letter to Andrew explaining that although he loved his books, he had failed to win the prize because his use of language didn't match his high standards of spiritual uplift. What a rebel my mum was dating.

Mal Duff sadly died at Everest Base Camp from a heart attack in 1997. It was a huge loss, felt heavily by Andrew, and I am still massively disappointed never to have met this extraordinary character. His friend Henry Todd was still running expeditions, and his camp happened to be just around the corner. It was the perfect place to start my inquiries. I had heard that Henry had once punched a cameraman, so hoped my connection to Andrew would keep me safe. With one last Mars bar and a gulp of tea, I gathered my kit and headed off with slight trepidation in the direction of Henry. Otherwise known as the Todd Father.

15

HENRY & THE COOK BOY

Henry's dome felt more like a palace than a tent. He had cosy rugs on the floor and his books, bed and bottles all neatly arranged like someone well used to camp life. With glasses slung round his neck and wearing a big woolly jumper, he looked friendly and at ease as he welcomed me in. 'Whisky?' he offered. Even though it was mid-afternoon, I thought what the hell and nodded enthusiastically. 'Very good.' With a grin, he poured me a generous double. I added in a little snow-ice and heard it crackle and hiss in the peaty amber dram. The rest of the afternoon was written off there and then.

I had a recording of Andrew Greig performing his poem *Back Again* live at the Queen's Hall in Edinburgh and I proudly played it to Henry. I glowed with pride as Henry closed his eyes.

We're back again with our tents, our trash, our high ambition
We've come to be both audience and show
Mal flicked his lighter. An avalanche roared
We've come to assert everything fits
And we believe the true scale of things
Is the entire mountain hung mirrored in our shades . . .

As the Edinburgh applause faded to the sound of our rustling tent, Henry opened his eyes with a smile. He was a big fan of

1   Dave prepares himself for the outrageously hard crux sequence of *Don't Die of Ignorance*, Ben Nevis, 2008. I was dangerously out of my depth as I tried to follow as a climbing cameraman. This ascent could have easily ended in tragedy.

2   Andrew Greig sings *Wild Mountain Thyme* at at our wedding in the woods. Just seven months after we started dating, new love and near death still fizzed like champagne in my veins and life felt too short to hold back.

3   Nature Girl Julie on our honeymoon in Tiree.

4   Filming from the Mittellegi Ridge, with the North Face of the Eiger behind. My camera is facing the wrong way and I nearly missed the all-important wingsuit flyby shot. Luckily Brian Hall filmed a backup. Phew.

5   Everest Geography from Pumori Base Camp, 2014. We were there to film a historic live broadcast of a BASE jump/ wingsuit flight from the summit (back left) to land at Base Camp below. The season ended in tragedy when 16 Sherpa were killed in the Khumbu Icefall (flowing like a frozen river through shot, moving up to three feet a day). This shot was taken before the avalanche and huge seracs on Everest's western shoulder can clearly be seen hanging above the Icefall.

6   Twelve tons of equipment to Base Camp. This was flown as far as Namche then took 300 porter loads and 400 yak loads to get it all to Base Camp. A single load for a porter is 30 KG – I've seen them carry double that while wearing flip-flops.

7   Andy Tyson's Solar Power System. Alpine Ascents still use this system today. The NBC Outside Broadcast rig can be seen on the right. NBC sent an incredibly hard working and talented team of technicians and producers to Base Camp.

8 My friend and guide Andy Tyson at Base Camp 2014. I was privileged to have him as my room mate and guide for this journey.

9 The NBC satellite rig was put to good use when Ed Wardle and Jonathon Fierro reported to the world that the Everest season was likely to be over. Ed was a great leader for the camera team as the tragedy unfolded. Matt Green is behind the camera

10 An estimated 10,400 cubic metres of snow and ice broke free after the 7.8m/w earthquake that hit Nepal on the 25th April 2015. The quake was so powerful Everest itself moved three centimetres south west. The huge avalanche fell for around one thousand metres before detonating on Base Camp with devastating force.

11 Left to Right: Dr David Fitzpatrick (USA), Vicky Hill (Scot/NZ), Rob Smith (Scot), Barry Smith (NZ) and Namgyal Sherpa enjoying drinks at the Adventure Consultants Puja ceremony. Namgyal Sherpa front left. The white on our faces is rice flour rubbed on to signify grey beards and long life.

12 Bright colours at Adventure Consultants camp before the avalanche. The white and red dining tent and smaller media tent can clearly be seen, with the green and yellow kitchen tent behind. Base Camp can be home to upwards of one thousand people at the peak of season. Luckily most were on the mountain when the avalanche happened.

13 Ground Zero. Dining tent can be seen inverted on the left, kitchen tent table exposed, and media tent destroyed. Anthea Fisher looks for her belongings in the background. It took days to find them.

14 Chhongba Sherpa was badly injured and couldn't remember who I was. I told him to rest here while we gathered the survivors and moved southwards to Himex and IMG camps where a field hospital and morgue had been set up.

15 My tent was launched 70ft down a rocky bank. Tent poles became spears and knives became missiles.

16 Taken by Sam Maynard as I handed over the rushes at Heathrow. I couldn't focus on anything for more than a few seconds at this point. The puja cords from the two tragic years can be seen round my neck. I didn't know if the Sherpa that tied them was alive or dead.

17 Home with my beloved girls Jemima (1) and Imogen (4). Julie had finished her cancer treatment just five months previously and had an agonising wait for news from me for the second year running. It had been a week since the avalanche. I was still wearing the same borrowed clothes from Base Camp.

18 I became obsessed with barefoot running and spent days, weeks, months creating trails through the forest with my dog Ziggy.

19 Cold water every day in the lochan. Always hard to get in, always feel better when I get out. This practice seems to create a space between me and my thoughts.

20 Chhongba Sherpa came all the way from his village, from Nunthala, to see me when I arrived in Kathmandu. I was overwhelmed by his kindness.

21 John Griber and I had become good friends in 2014 and he joined me again in 2016. Here he captures my mini-breakdown as I approach Base Camp and face my demons head on. I felt as if I was walking into the recurring nightmare I'd been having about my return to Base Camp and being buried again by another avalanche.

22 Helicopters were used for rescues and taxis from Base Camp. This is a B3e. There were different landing sites like these spread throughout Base Camp. I'd witnessed truly heroic flying from these pilots.

23

24

23 One of my favourite days at work ever. The summit of Lobuche East (6119m) with Everest in the background. I filmed my first Himalayan sunrise.

24 Greg Paul emerges from the Icefall like a high altitude whack-a-mole. I had to run into position and nearly missed the shot due to a wobbly lens.

25 Greg Paul and Ngawang Tenjing Sherpa on the summit of Everest. Greg Paul told me: *When I picture myself on the summit it is with Ngawang by my side. We were brothers on top of the world!*

26 Light Genies in the Valley of Silence – the Great Western Cmn. I sat watching wisps of light dance and twirl through icy air as I waited for the 2016 Himex team's triumphant return.

Andrew's work, but our connections didn't end there. Artist Rob Fairley, from Room 13, had also worked for Henry as a guide back in the eighties. To complete this web of association, Rob Fairley had gone to school with Mal Duff in Edinburgh. I tingled as I thought of all the events that had conspired over many years to bring me here, right now, clinking glasses with Henry. Or maybe that was the whisky? It was great to have a break from the constant pressure of filming and hang out and drink with an old friend that I'd only just met.

'It's like watching your children grow up,' Henry said as he leant forward to get the bottle. It was time for another wee dram. 'But you've got to be careful what you give birth to.' He had been part of the Everest scene since the beginning and was referring to what he was witnessing now as the industry grew around him. It was Henry, Mal Duff and Chowang Sherpa who took over the fixing of the Icefall from Adventure Consultants founder Rob Hall. This arrangement didn't last long because of Mal Duff's sudden death soon afterwards. Henry undertook the painful duty of getting Mal's body back to Kathmandu. That was a day when the climbing world lost one of a kind.

When Mal had started taking clients climbing in the late 1970s, it was purely a means to an end. Whether in Scotland, the Alps or the Himalayas he would bring clients along to pay for the trip. Both benefited: the client got a very real adventure and Mal got another route ticked off his wish list. Many a paying client could find themselves on a first ascent of a route on Ben Nevis or even on the Northeast Ridge of Everest for that matter. Mal didn't look for qualifications in the guides he employed, instead he looked for ability and knowledge. As the climbing industry became increasingly regulated in the UK, Mal was one of the last guides to be operating in this old school way. His approach didn't always go smoothly and Mal often had problems with finance, but he was a rebel and a dreamer whose free-spirited approach kick-started the careers of many fine climbers and enabled many others' dreams to come true.

As the industry was tightened up in the UK and Europe, Nepal remained free of such constraint. When Henry and Mal had started operating there were just a few companies guiding in the Himalayas. But all that had changed. Mallory's wildest dream of climbing Everest had become a common reality and Base Camp was heaving with new companies, many of whom didn't have the experience of the old guard. The trust that had existed between a few key players was still there, but with the slopes so saturated with novice climbers, it was no longer possible for them to manage the mountain in the same way.

Henry had mixed feelings about it all. Now an elder statesman of Base Camp, he had witnessed his employees grow and learn and gradually start to take the reins themselves, which was a good thing. What he hadn't envisioned was the direction in which the industry would grow and just how busy the slopes would become.

I was feeling quite drunk as I emerged from Henry's palace. Directly behind his camp, Pumori's mighty walls reared up steeply for almost a kilometre into the early evening sky. All along its vast ridge to neighbouring peak Lingtrin, was an impenetrable mosaic of cornices and seracs, hanging with serene menace and guarding the way to the summits beyond. I'd seen first-hand the devastation that had been caused when one of these had collapsed above the Icefall last year, but it was best not to think about that. In the other direction the summit of Everest was burning red and orange as the sun dipped on a fine afternoon. We stood together and took it all in. 'It's the closest you can get to the moon while still on earth,' Henry said with a twinkle as we shook hands, and I began my stagger towards my tent, Andrew's words echoing in my mind:

> *. . . from the heights we propose,*
> *to the depths we have left*
> *our shadows gestured and stretched.*

I was met with warm hellos and delicious food when I arrived back. It was clear to me why Adventure Consultants had such a great reputation. Their staff were happy, the expedition well-organised and the food was incredible. Tonight, it was my favourite: Tibetan momos, a dumpling-like savoury treat with various fillings that can either be deep fried or steamed.

I'd already had the pleasure of filming camp cook Dendi Sherpa and his younger brother Pemba as they showed off their culinary skills. 'I left the monastery to join my brother and work on the mountain this year,' grinned young Pemba as he washed vegetables in the bright afternoon sun. He had the first sprouts of stubble on his chin and keen enthusiasm in his eyes. Pemba had been training to be a monk, but left his maroon robes behind at the monastery for an old jacket and baseball cap. 'Maybe one day I will work on the slopes myself.'

This was a common progression for the Sherpa. Cook boy was an entry level job from which, with the right luck and attitude, you could go on to build a good career. Always smiling and ready to serve, Pemba's character was typical of most of the Sherpa that I met. The problem I could see from a TV perspective was that it was going to be a challenge to get beneath this natural tendency towards selflessness to find out their real opinions, not just the ones that they thought we wanted to hear.

Chhongba himself had been a cook boy. In 1990 he was invited to work in Colorado for a season. It was a big shock leaving his rural village with no electricity to find himself in American supermarkets 'with sliding doors and things'. He and his friend were housed in an apartment where for two days they didn't eat anything but a dry loaf of bread they found in the fridge as they didn't know how cook or work any of the appliances. When he went home to Nepal he vowed not to return to America until he had learned how to cook.

Chhongba had been involved in the trekking industry since he was a young boy. The late Rob Hall, founder of Adventure Consultants, was a big fan and even though he didn't have much experience in the kitchen, Rob offered him the role as camp cook. Chhongba politely declined at first, but Rob eventually persuaded him. The camp manager would write out recipes for Chhongba to follow and he did so diligently, sometimes adapting them for the environment and introducing new ideas like sushi or hot muffins. He soon established himself as Head Cook, a position he held for around twenty years. It is a role that involves a lot of planning and mathematics, skills that he has gone on to teach other cook boys as they have made their way up the ranks. This at times has been tricky. They often have no education, so he must start from scratch. Each food order must be around 30kg, a standard weight for a porter to carry. It can be frustrating as one year he may order a load of porridge that no one ends up eating, then the following year doesn't bother ordering the porridge and of course that's what everyone wants. One of Chhongba's most recognisable influences is the supply of hot steaming towels before each meal. It was an idea he got from a Thai Airways flight, that has now become standard practice throughout Base Camp and further down the valley.

The following days passed in a busy blur of introductions and meetings, storylines and shots. Raw TV didn't want me going off to Camp 2 with Garrett, so Chhongba and I got into our well-honed rhythm of daily camp visits and chats. Lou had made it home after a short stay in a Kathmandu hospital, where she was treated for AMS. I was checking in with her and Sandra in the office each day via satellite phone to let them know my progress and to check they were happy with what I was doing.

Our original schedule had a visit to Pumori Base Camp for us all on the 25th April, our penultimate day. I was excited about this as I'd been up once before. A two hour walk, directly behind and above Base Camp, it was a stunning spot. It gave the most incredible views right across into the Western Cmn and was the perfect place to get top shots of the geography of Base Camp. As the glacier had retreated over the years, Base Camp had been pushed further and further north to its current location right at the head of the valley. It was an accepted risk to camp here, and tents were set up well away from the giant walls of seracs, to give at least some sense of safety.

Although the abundance of luxuries made Base Camp a very comfortable setting, it was still an extremely wild place to be. The immense force of creation that thrust the ancient seabed of Everest to the sky in the first place continues, and the Himalayas creep ever upwards by over 1cm a year. What effect global warming will have remains to be seen. One thing is certain: as the temperature on Earth continues to rise, the permafrost that holds this relatively new mountain chain together will continue to melt. At some point in the future these mighty giants will surely start to shrink and crumble.

'This is a bad sign,' Chhongba warned. It was unnerving to see our peaceful, cheerful guide so concerned. Behind him lay a frozen web of Tibetan prayer flags, draped in icy tangles round our camp. Standing in his bright orange jacket, shaking his head with a frown, he was doing his best to rehang them. 'The gods must be unhappy,' he continued. I felt a shiver of fascination as he carefully untied a colourful knot of prayer flags wound round some kitchen utensils that had been left outside the cooking tent. What did he mean?

The flags had been erected during our Puja the previous day. Our ceremony had been particularly poignant as haunting memories of those we had lost in the Icefall avalanche the previous year were very much in our minds. Three Sherpa from Adventure Consultants' team had died that day. Juniper was burned, belongings blessed and mysterious Buddhist mantras chanted to appease unseen deities, somewhere above, controlling our fate.

That night, a fierce and scatty wind had descended abruptly on our camp, clawing at the fabric of our tents with unnerving aggression. It whipped all around, waking us, unsettling us, and leaving as quickly as it had arrived. With the coming of the first rays of sun, we could see that many of the prayer flags had been torn down and now lay in a multi-coloured tangle. Chhongba picked up a stray end that had been trampled into the snow. 'They must be unhappy,' he repeated, looking skyward to the summits, before turning to look at me.

16

EARTHQUAKE AVALANCHE

On the morning of the 25th April, I awoke feeling mentally tired, with characters and storylines all whizzing round my head with nowhere to go. I had spoken with Lou before bed and told her I was still planning to climb to Pumori Base Camp to get our 'top shots' in the morning. It was a good chance to stretch my legs and be a happy mountaineer for a few hours, rather than a stressed producer. As we spoke, I watched a plume of snow unwind from the roof of the world, while Lou balanced on a gate post in Wales, trying to get a signal. 'Don't go, Joe,' she told me clearly. 'We can get top shots of the camp from archive. Concentrate on your interviews instead.' I reluctantly agreed and could understand why they didn't want me wandering off on an adventure.

I unzipped my tent and peeked outside. Unusually low cloud was hanging, almost to the level of the glacier. The mountains were obscured, so there was no point heading up high anyway. I snuggled down, almost tempted to go back to sleep, but there were still a couple of important interviews that I needed to do, so I got myself up and ready to roll.

First, I would head to Alpine Ascents camp, to find Lakpa Rita Sherpa at the top end of Base Camp, right beneath the Icefall. Although I'd said hello and spent time with him during this trip, I hadn't pulled my camera out as I was waiting for the right time. Today felt like the right day for that. In the afternoon I would then visit Dr Rachel Tullet and her colleague Dr Megan Walmsley at Everest ER. I'd enjoyed hanging out with them, but again hadn't done any filming, even though an agreement in principle was in place to do so.

There had been a warm, well-organised atmosphere when I visited their ER tent, right in the heart of Base Camp. Rachel, in a turquoise puffa jacket with her shoulder length brown hair popping out below her beanie, had a quick-fire brain, full of curiosity and enthusiasm. She had worked regularly for Medecins Sans Frontieres and was always busy, even when no patients were present. The bond between her and her colleague Meg was obvious, and they worked brilliantly together, smoothly and efficiently. The two of them, along with their Nepalese colleague Dr Aditya, dealt with everything from coughs and cuts to full blown medical emergencies. I was very wary of getting my camera out at the wrong time and creating an uncomfortable atmosphere. I sensed they were wary of me as well.

Everest ER was set up by American doctor Luanne Freer in 2003 for the good of everyone at Base Camp. Working closely with the Himalayan Rescue Association (HRA), the clinic provided free treatment for the Sherpa and porters, subsidised by money generated through the treatment of westerners in need of medical attention. To work there as a doctor, you first had to work for a season at one of the HRA clinics in Pheriche or Manang. It was a highly sought-after role and there was a long waiting list of adventurous medics waiting for the opportunity. It was, and is, a truly wonderful organisation who not only provide vital medical services, but also generate a sense of a community and togetherness among all the politics that can be found at Base Camp. No matter who you are, a poor porter with snow blindness or a rich climber with cerebral or pulmonary oedema, you can receive first-class treatment from the dedicated professionals who work there.

Everest ER was used to being the focus of media attention. Although this could be a positive thing and the publicity generated could be very helpful, there was a flip side. I got a sense straight away that the staff certainly didn't want to be part of a production that was full of heightened drama and jeopardy.

I felt caught between two worlds. On the one hand I was there to develop a TV show and knew the kind of storylines we would be looking for, but on the other, outside of my role as a producer, I completely understood their concerns about their professional roles being turned into the subject of entertainment TV. Striking the balance for us all was going to be a challenge and access had to be based upon trust and trust needed to be earned. I was quite stressed at being in the middle and hoped my reassurances about the integrity of our show turned out to be true.

An oppressive atmosphere seemed to hang over the Alpine Ascents camp as I approached. Not only had they lost five Sherpa the previous year, but this year's team were also coming to terms with the devastating news of Andy Tyson's passing. I felt subdued as I made my way through the tents, some of which I recognised. This year the camp was small and discrete, with only a handful of clients, a far cry from the media circus we had created a year ago.

Andy's friend and fellow guide Eric Murphy greeted me with a welcoming hug. He was sorting his kit out for the mountain and keen to speak about a suitable time to hold a Puja or some sort of ceremony for Andy. With so many folk already climbing, waiting till after the first round of rotations seemed to be a good plan. Chhongba had taken it upon himself to arrange for some prayer flags to be blessed for the occasion and there were a lot of people at Base Camp who wanted to pay their respects.

The humble and legendary Lakpa Rita then appeared from his tent carrying a brew and, with silent flakes of snow falling all around, gave me the most moving of interviews. In his green down jacket, his deep hazel eyes glistening with emotion, he told me about his experience the previous year.

'I found eleven dead bodies all in the same spot,' he started, then paused. Snow was landing and melting on the rim of his cap. 'And pretty much dug them all out.' I wondered if it was wrong of me to have asked the question, but he seemed okay to talk about it. 'Since seeing all of this,' he continued, 'I decided not to climb . . . something doesn't feel right inside and whatever you feel inside, you have to listen to yourself.'

Tears were burning my cheeks as he spoke. Real wisdom comes from experience, and this had a particular resonance. I felt privileged to be hearing this softly spoken man. He had made a promise to his wife not to climb any more and instead stayed behind as Base Camp Manager this year. He had well and truly earned this right after 36 expeditions and 17 summits.

Lakpa Rita had seen massive changes at Base Camp since he started as a climbing Sherpa in 1984. Back then there were usually just a few teams, nothing like what Everest had become today. After the disaster of 1996, where eight people lost their lives on the mountain, he had thought this growing industry might have died down, but the opposite had happened. Things got even busier. He had an interesting idea of how the Ministry of Tourism could manage the crowds. If they required climbers to have experience of summiting another 8000m peak before attempting Everest, it would spread the load to lesser visited peaks and keep Everest's slopes clear of the inexperience that jeopardises everyone's safety. Like Henry Todd, he had seen the industry grow from humble beginnings into the beast it had become.

At the end of our interview, we hugged then drank tea together quietly. His radio blared with updates from the mountain. Ben Jones was guiding a group up there somewhere in the clouds, while Eric prepared himself for the next round of rotations. As we said goodbye, I felt warmed by being with Lakpa. Despite all the suffering, life carries on. All we can do is support each other and keep moving forward.

Wandering back to my camp, my mind full of the previous year's events, I sat on a rock to give me time to think. I didn't want to rush back but instead let Lakpa Rita's softly spoken words settle. The interview had stirred me deeply. A chance to talk things through with him was one of the reasons I had chosen to come back. I was pleased to have finally thanked him for all that he had selflessly done for everyone, alive and dead, the previous year. I'd been thinking about doing so ever since I had left without the chance to say a proper goodbye.

The clouds were still hanging low, thick and heavy. Base Camp was relatively quiet as most climbers were acclimatising somewhere above. Perched on this rock, on this mighty glacier, beneath this mighty mountain, was the perfect place to think about this mighty man. What a crazy world Lakpa Rita was involved in up here in the clouds.

I hadn't walked far from my perch when a wave of animal prickles swept across my skin. My senses knew something that my mind did not. The ice beneath my feet juddered, then cracked and hissed. I swayed as if I was at sea. Then it stopped. I looked up to see a figure running from the Icefall towards Base Camp and grabbed for my camera. A deep, thunderous roar began to echo all around. It was impossible to locate, but it was growing louder, as if the mountains were collapsing above me. As I found my frame, I noticed the same figure turning 180° and running back the way he came. I hit record and panned round.

The low grey cloud hanging above Base Camp began to expand violently. What the hell was I filming? Explosions of snow, ice, rock and debris were all churning together into one enormous blast right over our camp. I was so mesmerised by my shot, for a moment it didn't seem real. Then it burst out of my frame into reality. Instinctively I started to run, though it was pointless. The glacier was bare. There was nowhere to hide.

My camera was still rolling as I looked back over my shoulder. I heard myself cry out as Base Camp began disappearing under a dark shroud, expanding ever upwards and outwards. Within seconds the fierce shock wave had hit me and I was blown off my feet. As I crouched over my camera, something screamed past my head, and I braced myself for impact. This was it. Breathe, focus, breathe. Gasping and choking among howling waves of snow, ice and grit, I cut the camera.

I was swallowing the mountain and it was expanding into my lungs, throat and nose. Beginning to suffocate, I didn't know if my eyes were open or closed. All I could see were white fuzzy dots, grey fuzzy dots, everywhere and in everything. Part of my mind was ablaze with a million thoughts all at once. I wasn't ready to die. But I had to be brave. I had to die well. But my girls, my girls. How could this be happening?

Simultaneously, another part of me was becoming increasingly detached. I felt the same shift of perspective I'd experienced on *Don't Die*, as if bursting through my seams once more. It was no longer just me gasping for air on the glacier. It was me *and* the awareness of me gasping for air on the glacier. I was witness to it all from a place beyond my terrified, cartwheeling mind. Time started to fragment. My body heaved and gasped for air, but as I struggled, I felt an increasing sense of calm emerging, overriding the panic. I tried to put all my attention there, knowing that one way or another this ever-expanding moment of suffocation would have to let go of me. Then suddenly it did.

I choked in the silence that descended as abruptly and as violently as the avalanche had exploded, and finally got a thin sliver of breath. *I'm alive. I think.* I hacked and spluttered my lungs into action again, feeling the deep burn of exploded mountain being expelled from my lacerated airways. I picked and peeled my frozen eyelids open, only to be blinded by bright grey stillness, my eyeballs full of scratches and grit and trying to settle on something. The sensation of being witness still lingered as I pulled myself out of my shallow grave and dusted myself down, shaking and squinting, trying to find centre and sense. Eventually my stinging eyes found focus on the devastation that camp had become and from somewhere deep within a primal wail of emotion arose and broke away from me. I staggered a few steps towards camp and fell over again. Rags of canvas hung deadly still in post-catastrophic silence.

Fifty feet or so away, two figures lay in front of me twitching violently, eyes rolling back and groaning, dying, their naked torsos smearing the ice in blood. They looked as if they had been picked up and thrown down a bank through a cheese grater of rocks and ice that had ripped off their clothes and smashed their heads. 'Put some clothes on,' I instructed, unable to process what I was seeing. I felt quite cross with them for being so poorly dressed. 'You will be okay, but please try and be still and you must put some clothes on.' They continued to spasm, making noises I'd never heard before. 'I will get help; don't worry, I will get help.' I took a few steps away. *'Please help me someone!'* I was now witness again to my shouts and unnerved by the unfamiliar tone in my voice. Why was no one coming? Why won't they be still? 'Please somebody help us, we've got two dying here, I need help. Please someone. *For God's sake I need help!'*

I started to feel angry that no one was coming and that I had a camera in my bag, and I was there to make a documentary and I hated that fact, and I didn't know what to do. Crying and still annoyed with them, I told them I'd be back and then left them there convulsing. Two bleeding bodies burning on the ice. There was nothing I could do.

Keeping my camera in the bag, I headed back in the direction of camp, calling for help the whole way. As I drew closer, I started to realise why no one had come. I was walking into an apocalypse. Everything was smashed and broken. Our camp was no longer there. Zombies were staggering, some made unrecognisable by blood and injury. One of our young kitchen staff, Ang Thili, had half his face hanging off, exposing his eye socket and cheek bone. Chhongba was limping round in circles, caked in blood and down feathers, unable to recognise me.

Anthea Fisher hugged me as I stumbled back into camp. Dr Dave confessed to thinking I was dead. My tent had been hurled at least 70ft, before smashing into rocks down the steep banking in front of camp. The same bank the porters had been blown off. Some of my belongings had stayed inside while others had been scattered or buried, never to be found again. Our whole camp was destroyed, crushed, ripped and torn to shreds. There were numerous dead but at this point we were unsure exactly how many. Anthea had been dozing in her tent when the earthquake struck. She'd jumped out and was on the radio to Suze up at Camp 1 immediately. They were okay up there but concerned about what was going on at Base Camp. Then the roar of collapsing seracs started to echo down. She came out of the comms tent to see what was happening and, to her horror, the cloud directly above her tore apart. Chhongba pointed to the dining tent. Vicky Hill and Dr Dave ran inside. Anthea didn't want to join them in case she became trapped. What to do? The double framed vestibule of the dining tent could be a better option. She jumped in, just as it hit. Huddled in the vestibule, Anthea battled for breath as she inhaled wave after wave of gritty, icy debris. There was no oxygen left in the air to breathe. She began to think how ironic it was that she was to die like this. She had been teaching avalanche awareness courses in New Zealand just before she had come to Everest.

Under the sudden and awful weight of grief, reality became a thick soup. I was wading from one terrible scene to another. I couldn't quite process what I was looking at, though from the tripod legs sticking out of the snow, I realised what I was standing in was the mangled remains of our media tent. There was no canvas left, just twisted tent poles and an exposed wooden base, half buried in snow. It now seemed extraordinary that Sam and Lou had already been airlifted out. I'm sure one, if not all of us, would have been in there as it was blown away.

I didn't know if the items of clothing sticking out of the snow had bodies attached to them or not. I tugged at a few pieces, unsure of what might appear as I continued to wander around in shock, grief, and guilty relief.

From round the corner Henry Todd staggered through the low mist, like a wounded soldier from *Apocalypse Now*. He was clutching a hugely swollen left hand. 'Henry, my God, are you okay?' I burst into tears as he hugged me. Both of us had presumed the other one must be dead. 'I'd just left my tent to deliver an oxygen regulator to Jagged Globe,' he said, shivering, 'then I ducked behind the Puja Altar when it came.' This had somehow been enough to save both him and the man he'd pulled beside him, just in the nick of time. Henry had lost three of his men. Two of them had somehow been blown into our camp, such was the force of the blast. He had come to find oxygen as his camp no longer existed. Suddenly, Anthea, who had just joined us, picked up a regulator that was lying at her feet among a great jumble of other stuff. 'Here you go,' she said matter-of-factly.

In the same strange way as I'd felt cross with the two dying porters for not having clothes on, Anthea told me later how she had felt similarly cross with Henry's men for coming to our camp to die. She had enough of her own dying people in camp to deal with.

Henry was shaking and distant but keeping it together. He needed stretchers to be made from tent poles and torn fabric, to move his men. 'I feel so frustrated I can't do more,' he said, looking down at his swollen, bluish hand. He told me later that when I had met him, he had just come off the phone to Garrett Madison. He'd had to pass on some devastating news. Like most guides, Garrett was up on the mountain with his clients for their first round of rotations. Marisa Eve Girawong, his girlfriend and expedition doctor, had died at his camp.

17

A QUESTION OF ETHICS

Anthea Fisher had well and truly taken charge. I could see why Guy Cotter wanted her as Base Camp Manager. She had heard that the south end of Base Camp, about a kilometre away, had not been hit by the blast. She was good friends with the guides at Himalayan Experience (Himex), whose camp had not been affected, and knew that was probably the best direction for us to head in. Anthea and Vicky had been partying in the huge Himex dome tent the previous night. Anthea had been dozing off a hangover when the earthquake hit.

All we could do was round up anyone who was still alive and stagger down in that direction to assess what to do next. 'You need to start walking!' Anthea forcibly instructed the stunned and injured Sherpa we had gathered. They looked at her blankly. Chhongba still didn't know who I was and was muttering strange words to himself, blood oozing from his head and also beginning to soak through his trousers.

With everyone rounded up, our caravan of survivors began limping southwards. Vicky Hill had lost her shoes and was wearing an oversized pair of men's trainers she'd found in the snow. Ang Thili was hanging from one of her arms and another badly injured Sherpa clung to the other. I was propping Chhongba up, repeating, 'It will all be okay,' in my mind or out loud, over and over. I didn't know if it would be. After a while Chhongba got into a rhythm and seemed okay to hobble by himself. Up to that point every time I let go, he had just started walking in circles. I kept an eye on him, but helped Vicky, who, despite sliding around in her boat-like trainers, was doing incredibly well.

We stared in disbelief as we passed Garrett's camp. It had also taken a direct hit and was in a similar state to ours. With everybody stunned and blood-soaked, the usual twenty-five minute walk to Himex took us closer to an hour. One step at a time. As we made progress down it became clear to us that our camps must have been at the epicentre of the blast. The further away we got, the less obvious the damage. Then, weirdly, there was no damage at all.

Outside Himex's camp, I screamed at someone pointing a professional camera at us. 'Put that fucking camera down and go and help, there's people dying up there!' I was shocked at the fury in my own voice. I think his presence must have emphasised my own internal conflict. Seeing him film us made me question whether I too should be trying to film. Amongst the chaos, it was hard to think straight. Having a camera in my bag was a huge extra stress. This poor bloke, to whom I apologised later, had no idea what we had emerged from. He was just doing his job.

When we got to Himex, we were diverted to International Mountain Guides' (IMG) camp next door. It had become a makeshift field hospital and morgue in a very short space of time. There, I became witness to one of the most extraordinary displays of leadership, organisation and group strength in adversity that it was possible to imagine. It made me proud to be a member of the human race. Base Camp was pulling together to deliver an outstanding humanitarian effort. And we needed it.

Greg Vernovage, IMG's expedition leader, and Sirdar Ang Jang Bu, calmly directed us to where we ought to be. Their steady authority and leadership were exactly what we needed. Vicky and I delivered our men to where we were told to take them, then we stopped and stared at each other. My mouth and lips were burning with acid. She was covered in blood. We were both shaking as we hugged.

Pretty soon IMG's tents became full of doctors and guides from across Base Camp, all focused on the work of saving people's lives. Himex's doctor, Anne Brance, was in the thick of it all, already making sense of who needed to be where and what needed to be done, again with countless others, whose names I don't know. They were helping people suffering the most horrendous injuries. It was clear from the amount of head trauma that the damage was more like that of a bomb blast than a traditional avalanche.

We later learned that the earthquake had triggered a huge serac to collapse from the col between Pumori and Lingtrin, maybe around 10,400 cubic metres of snow and ice. It had dropped a thousand metres, gathering up everything in its path, before exploding like a shrapnel bomb on the centre of Base Camp. As well as all the debris from the mountain smashing through the air, tent poles had become deadly spears and kitchen knives had become missiles. It was just luck whether you missed the impact or not. It was later estimated that the first wave of the blast was travelling at somewhere between three hundred and five hundred kilometres an hour as it hit Base Camp. It was this shock wave that had caused so much devastation.

Because of the low cloud, we knew it would be impossible to get the much-needed helicopters up there to help us. We were on our own, cut off from the old world and locked into this dreadful new one. Thank goodness there were so many skilled people up there able and willing to help. Through their brilliance we were at least bringing some order to the chaos and undoubtedly many lives were saved that would otherwise have been lost. I delivered

Chhongba to the tent for the seriously injured who hopefully weren't fatally wounded. It was so hard to tell.

I must have looked in a sorry state when I bumped into Henry Todd again as he ordered me to sit down and drink some tea. 'You look awful, Joe; you need to stop!' he commanded. I huddled in next to him and sat for a moment, overwhelmed by uncontrollable shaking. I snuggled in close, feeling comforted by his presence. My throat felt as if it had been ripped by thousands of tiny razor blades and I was oscillating between being present to all that was going on and then becoming completely detached from it. God knows how everyone was managing to work so professionally through all this. I was shell-shocked.

As I slowly sipped sweet tea, I started to come round and tuned into the conversation. Nepal had been hit by a massive earthquake measuring 7.8Mw on the Richter scale. The epicentre was around one hundred and fifty miles from us, and the country had been devastated. Whole villages vanished under landslides, ancient temples crumbled to the ground, thousands were dead, thousands injured, and thousands made homeless. We had no idea how many had lost their lives at Base Camp, but it looked upwards of twenty. It was of a scale I couldn't comprehend. Nepal had declared a national emergency.

'I think I might have filmed it coming through the clouds,' I whispered to Henry. 'Really?' His eyes were wide and serious. I pulled my icy camera out of my rucksack and my quivering hands scraped the viewfinder clean. The camera was still working, but only just. We sat in silence as we watched the forty seconds or so of footage that I had got before cutting the camera. I didn't want to show anyone else the footage. Despite being an emotional wreck and shaking so badly I could barely hold the camera, I still had that nagging voice somewhere inside telling me to get back to work. The camera was caked in ice, and I didn't know where my spare batteries were, but nevertheless the voice was still there. Perhaps I should be filming all this? Perhaps I will ruin my reputation as a good producer if I don't? That other guy was filming, why wasn't I?

This caused a whole lot of extra conflict and turmoil inside my already beleaguered brain. My gut instinct was to help where I could, but now I'd got everyone down to IMG's camp, perhaps I should get back to work? I was almost crying at the thought, but with some sweet tea inside me and reassurance from Henry, I started to feel a little stronger.

I took a deep breath, which hurt, and put my rucksack back on. I would search for any spare medical supplies in the wreckage and bring them down to the expanding field hospital the IMG camp was becoming. While there, I would also get some shots of our camp and the surrounding area to document the end of this tragic journey. I could also use the walk as a way of trying to pull my head back together. What about Julie and the kids? What about all my family? They must have heard about this by now. Did they even know if I was alive?

Just outside camp I bumped into Lakpa Rita, carrying oxygen bottles. Thank God he was alive, thank God I was alive. The interview I had done with him not two hours before seemed to have taken place in a different world. It could well have saved my life. 'You okay, mate?' We embraced, our eyes full of tears. He nodded. 'You okay too?' I nodded back. We paused for a moment, holding each other's elbows, then turned and carried on our separate missions. There was nothing more to say.

I couldn't quite process what I was seeing when I arrived back where our camp had been. Neither could Vicky Hill, who'd come back to try and find some of her belongings. Wide eyed, her ashen face peeping out of her hood revealed just how upset she was. Her tent had been picked up and thrown so violently that it had ended up squeezed between two boulders that were only centimetres apart. Behind her lurked the half-submerged, mangled frame of the dining tent. Everything was everywhere. So were we.

I plucked up the courage to get the camera out of my bag. 'I better get some shots of this,' I said flatly, 'so they can see what happened.' Vicky nodded in silent agreement. I tried to shoot but couldn't settle on a shot for more than a couple of seconds. It didn't seem real. I was twitching from one scene of destruction to another, just like my brain as it galloped between thoughts. Perhaps an explanation was needed. Could I ask Vicky? Should I ask Vicky? Having just experienced having a camera pointed at me and the fury it had unleashed, I now knew how it felt to be the subject of a shot I didn't want to be in. Was this different?

Vicky and I were friends and I felt she trusted me. I felt a sudden surge of adrenaline. The words, 'Can you explain what happened?' came out of my mouth. 'Sure,' she nodded. With a pounding heart, I turned the camera on her.

'We're currently standing in the centre of what was our camp . . .' she began, then paused to wipe her eyes and became more distant. 'There's bodies . . . I'm very lucky.' I held my shot on her face. I felt I was intruding but had to stay committed to the moment now it had begun. The camera became a brief barrier to reality. I needed a cutaway. I panned from her tears onto the mangled remains of the dining tent behind her. 'I can't believe you survived in there. It's all so fucked up,' I said. Most of it was under snow, crumpled and piled in on itself beyond recognition. Expedition barrels had been emptied out and belongings strewn everywhere.

'I managed to find a channel on the edge that wasn't flattened . . .' Vicky continued, then paused again. 'I crawled out along that . . . ten metres away one of the Sherpa didn't make it . . .' I switched the camera off and joined her in our numb reality again. Pure chance had kept us both alive, but not others. I didn't know how many of our team had died. It was too much to comprehend.

Later, she told me how she'd ended up in the middle of the dining tent. The blast had wrapped the tent over itself side on, so the ceiling had become the floor. Somehow the tables inside had formed a barrier that had protected her from most of the impact, but then snow poured in from every direction. She thought that was how she was going to die. Once she'd crawled out along her narrow channel, she could hear Dr Dave calling for help from the far side of the tent. He'd become trapped under the twisted tent canvas and needed help to get out.

Our kitchen tent had been crushed and spun into an awful whirlpool of knives and noodles, blood and biscuits, all mashed together in an icy pulp. Hooded figures wandered and picked among the wreckage as the eerie silence hummed around them. I could see Anthea Fisher making her way towards me and with the camera still in my hands, I must have instinctively slipped back into TV mode. I lifted it up and started rolling again. I could do this, get some actuality, construct a scene. It's what I was good at. Anthea seemed okay with this, but I soon realised I wasn't. 'I can't find a thing of my own,' she told me. 'Not one thing.' Her tent had been vapourised. It ended up taking days to find. After a moment's discomfort, I dropped the camera and left it recording my feet. The barrier it created between me and her and what had happened was too much. I needed to be present and processing not zooming and focusing.

'We've lost four,' Anthea told me. The weight of our new reality swept over me, and I had to sit down. 'What here, at this camp?' *No.* This couldn't be happening again. One of them was Pemba

Sherpa, the young cook boy. He had been in the kitchen tent and been found underneath his friend Ang Thili. They had been huddled together when it struck.

In my torn state, I wandered off and turned the camera on myself. I melted down completely. Smaller avalanches continued to fall, breaking the silence with a rumble and a whoomph. 'I've just found out we've lost four of our Sherpa,' I wept. The sight of my pasty, trembling self in the viewfinder and the sound of my breaking voice made me weep even more. 'I'm just so lucky I wasn't in my tent,' I continued, 'otherwise I'd be dead right now.' Saying this out loud made the reality of it even more shocking. I confessed the feelings of conflict I was experiencing towards filming and tried to make clear to whoever would be watching the rushes, just how appalling the whole situation was.

The final death count at Base Camp was twenty-two. Six of those were our friends at Adventure Consultants, all of whom were from our Sherpa team: Dawa Tsering Sherpa, Pema Yishi Sherpa, Chhimi Dawa Sherpa, Pemba Sherpa, Maila Rai and Jangbu Sherpa, who died later in hospital.

I couldn't find any medical supplies at our camp, so I headed towards Everest ER, where I thought there must be plenty. I prayed that they'd missed the main pulse of the avalanche. They hadn't. I arrived to find a scene of absolute horror.

Doctor Rachel Tullet had survived the blast but was injured and limping around bodies heaped on the ground. When she had heard the earthquake, she'd headed out of the tent, looking in the direction of the Icefall, thinking the sound may have been coming from there. Rachel and Meg had been up all night looking after a patient suffering from cerebral oedema. She had just been evacuated when another sick patient from Base Camp arrived needing emergency treatment. Their first concern was for him. Meg stayed with the patient as Rachel ventured out to investigate the noise. Then the sky above her exploded. Rachel instinctively started to run but the force of the blast picked her up and threw her over a ridge, smashing her leg and covering her in suffocating debris. Somehow, she survived.

Both Rachel's watch and radio were lost. There was no sense of time. There was devastation all around and casualties soon started to arrive. As they did, the ER team began triaging them into their relevant group of injured, critically injured, or dead. Rachel's face was white, her eyes wide, but she was completely focused and in control when I arrived. She was working outside while Meg somehow continued to work within the wreckage of the tent. I can only describe it as a warzone.

Despite being injured and under the most unbelievable pressure, Rachel remained calm, giving clear direction to others, while dealing with endless scenes of suffering. Everywhere you looked there were bodies and the smell of blood permeated everything. Unbelievably, the team were managing to find life-saving supplies among the wreckage and deliver the emergency treatments needed.

The risk of further avalanches and aftershocks was very high. Once all the casualties local to the area had been located, Rachel and Greg Vernovage began making plans for a mass evacuation down to his IMG's camp. It would take a lot of manpower and time to carry everyone and everything down to the far end of Base Camp, well over a kilometre away. Everyone who could help was needed. Guides Mike Hamill, Mark Tucker and Willie Benegas were heavily involved in all this, as well as countless others whose names I don't know. The heroic doctors, guides, Sherpa and climbers who helped that day ended up being responsible for saving more than twenty lives. The most terrible circumstances brought about the very best in human nature and the level of dedication and skill I was witness to was awe-inspiring. It also left me with a stressful dilemma.

When Rachel first saw me arrive at ER, I could see what she was thinking. We both knew I had a camera in my bag. I was being paid by Discovery to be there. There was a split second to decide. Do I film or do I help? Sounds straightforward, but with so many demons in my head, it was hard to think straight. 'Brilliant,' a voice whispered, encouraging me to film, 'what a scene!' It was the same voice that got excited about the missing climbers on Annapurna. Rachel held my gaze for a second, as if she was reading me. How could I trust that voice? I had to trust my heart. It was telling me to help. If I were a journalist, perhaps my instincts would have been different. But I wasn't. I was a climber from Sheffield, living a dream that had become a nightmare. I gave Rachel a big hug and told her what an amazing job she was doing. We were both trembling.

Her colleague Lakpa Norbu Sherpa did need my help. There were two corpses that needed packing up and carrying to the helipad. He was struggling to find enough people to help. I had interviewed Lakpa at the beginning of the trip – he often worked with Simrik helicopters and had been one of the lone shadows we saw soaring through the sky the previous year, as he accompanied the corpses on the end of a longline. He survived this year's disaster by jumping behind a rock as thousands of tons of mountain exploded all around him.

I recognised the dead men. They were the two porters I had come across in the immediate aftermath of the quake. They had lost their battle and now needed to be wrapped in blue tarpaulins. The problem Lakpa was having was finding enough people willing to help, as it wasn't just their physical bodies we were dealing with. In Tibetan Buddhist belief it is thought that the soul of the newly deceased can linger around its former body for some time before it starts its long journey towards its next incarnation. It is common practice to avoid disturbing the corpse until all the warmth has left the body, to avoid interfering with the complex shift in dimension the soul is adjusting to. Aware of these beliefs, I understood the natural hesitation from some Sherpa about getting involved with wrapping the bodies.

The porters' stiffened bodies were smearing the blue tarpaulin purple with blood as we packaged them up. Their eyes remained frozen open, as if transfixed by the new realm they were entering. Once wrapped and covered we carried them towards the helicopter pad and left them there until they could be moved. I whispered an explanation and offered some kind words of consolation to any lingering souls who may be listening. I then swayed and stumbled my way back down to camp.

18

LONG JOURNEY HOME

IMG's camp was even busier by the time I got back. I spotted Dr Dave's silver hair as he hurried past, clutching medical supplies on his way to one of the tents. To my immense relief Chhongba had stabilised and recognised me as soon as I knelt next to him with some water. He had no recollection of the blast. His hip was badly injured, but his head wounds were thankfully mostly superficial. Coming round in that tent must have been frightening. There were four seriously injured people inside, all making haunting sounds. It was uncomfortably hot, bright and stuffy – thick with the smells of blood and burst down feathers.

A man next to us was writhing in agony, gibbering and moaning. I offered him some water, but he shook his head and clutched at his penis. I guessed the poor guy needed to pee but couldn't move or control his body. I took a deep breath, pulled the ripped red crust of his trousers back, held his penis into the cup and hoped for the best. The few brown drops that eventually dribbled out missed the cup and stung my grazed fingers. I went outside to wipe my hands clean in the snow outside, breathing deeply – which still hurt.

Russell Brice's Himex camp was next door and fast becoming an overflow for the expanding hospital. The cloud was still down, and it was certain there would be no helicopter assistance that day. Russell's huge dome tent was becoming a refugee centre, filling up with the homeless and injured from all around camp. They let me use their satellite phone, so I was eventually able to call Julie.

'My darling, I'm so sorry,' I blubbered. The sound of her concerned voice was enough to tip me over the edge. For the second year running I found myself making this call, apologising for putting her through all this.

'My God, don't be silly love, thank God you're okay. Are you okay?' I could barely hold the phone to my mouth and was finding it difficult to form a coherent sentence, gibbering from one subject to the next. 'I think so,' I told her, but honestly, I didn't know.

The night that followed was one of the toughest I have ever experienced. Himex's dome became home for forty or so of us, all suffering various degrees of trauma and all dealing with it accordingly. Some sobbing gently, some weeping inconsolably, some shouting out and shrieking, some staring silently at the condensation dripping down the canvas walls. After making sure that Chhongba would be okay for the night, I tried to settle down myself.

Avalanches were still falling all around and with every rumble came a fresh pang of fear. Anthea and Vicky were spooned on a sofa bed together and I was next to them on some cushions. Sleep was out of the question. To think they were partying here less than twenty-four hours before. At best I was able to steady my breathing and heart rate for a while, but then would lose my rhythm again. All the images of the day raced uncontrollably around the merry-go-round of my mind. At one point I needed a pee and had to clamber across everyone to get out. The sweep from my head-torch illuminated dozens of wide eyes staring at nothing but the darkness inside.

~

Eventually the first glimmers of light started to pierce through the canvas to free us from this long night, so at least we could now share our struggles with one another again. Then we heard a noise. I was standing just outside the tent when I first heard it. A delicate hum and echo for a second, then it was gone. I moved further from the camp, wondering if I was hearing things. But thankfully I wasn't. There it was again. This time a little louder and consistent in its frequency. My heart lifted with my eyes to the sky as I realised what it must be.

A helicopter! I stood with my attention transfixed at the point where the Khumbu glacier ends at Lobuche, until eventually I got a glimpse of it buzzing into view. I felt a buzz too. As it flew closer and closer, its buzzing developed into a triumphant roar. The blades beating the sky seemed to proclaim that hope and help were now here. Cries of relief echoed round the camp as we collectively gathered outside to watch it land.

The efforts of everyone who had helped so many to survive through that night were remarkable. It would be hard to imagine more horrific and challenging circumstances to be presented with and the selfless brilliance of those involved was heroic.

As one helicopter turned to three, then four, we could finally start the process of getting everybody out, eighteen hours or so after the quake had hit. Dr Rachel Tullet, Dr Anne Brance and others had prepared an order of evacuation, which accounted for seventy or so patients who had been stabilised at the makeshift field hospital overnight. First to go were the most seriously injured and in need of more sophisticated care. Chhongba was included in this, and I was so pleased to see him hobble on board, though I didn't get a chance to say goodbye. The whole country had been devastated by the quake, including many of the hospitals in Kathmandu, so it wouldn't be a straightforward journey for him or anyone.

The helicopters also had another mission as many climbers and guides were now stuck up at Camps 1 and 2. They were unable to come back down through the Icefall as the route had been destroyed. Remarkably, despite being bombarded with avalanches themselves, there had been nothing on the scale that had hit us and everyone, although petrified, had survived uninjured. They had to listen to events unfold by radio, unable to do anything but wait and hope that the same wasn't about to happen to them. Once the badly injured had been evacuated from Base Camp, the helicopters started clearing Camps 1 and 2. The air was alive with a continuous flow of helicopters, circling, landing and taking off again.

The competition for the helicopters was fierce. I knew that Raw TV and Discovery were working hard to get me out of there, but I was happy to take my place at the back of the queue. So many people were in greater need.

Back at Adventure Consultants' camp, I waited patiently and sifted through the wreckage for anything that was salvageable. My tent had been squashed, bent double and thrown 70ft or so from where it had started. Some of my possessions remained inside, some had obviously travelled a lot further. I spent the morning searching, contemplating my good luck and others' misfortune. One moment I would be okay, the next I'd be all over the place and have to stop and sit down. There was still a constant shiver vibrating though my veins. How on earth had I survived?

Pumori's wall of death stood behind the camp, its cliffs scoured clean by the blast and now gleaming in the bright blue morning sky. How deadly beautiful it was. I began stressing about the conflict I felt about filming the previous day. Would I have to explain my actions? Would Discovery understand? Had I just blown my career? I had a GoPro in my pocket, so did a little filming among the jumble of chaos, which eased this stress a little. One small consolation as I searched among the wreckage was that I couldn't find the hard drive with the dodgy helicopter rushes I had shot at the beginning of the trip. All that unnecessary stress was now buried forever.

My willingness to wait patiently for my helicopter ride wasn't shared by everyone. In fact, some awful behaviour was starting to emerge. It was clear that for the second year running there would be no climbing on the mountain. Clients from other camps that hadn't been affected started to descend, wanting to get the hell out of there. Greg Vernovage and others continued to do a great job managing this, but with so much going on, it was hard to keep the chancers at bay.

The demand and pressure on flights was so high that the helicopters were being refuelled with their blades still turning. While people clambered on board, the groundman would quickly empty his jerry can of fuel inside, then run for cover as it lurched back into the thin air to start another round of rescues. Again, I was witness to incredible levels of skill on display by some of the world's most composed and skilful pilots, as they calmly went about the business of rescuing and saving us. If it wasn't for them, it would have been a different story altogether.

I eventually heard that my name was on the list for the next flight, along with a producer working for the BBC called Tom Martienssen. He had just been flown down from Camp 1 and although we were happy to see each other, we were also a little concerned about the flight ahead of us. All the seats of the helicopter had been taken out, so it was just a metal shell, and before we set off the pilot had to ask me to move my leg so he could get full movement of his main control lever. With a few worrying lurches, we eventually took off and flew down the valley, first to Pheriche, then onwards to Lukla where the airport was. Thankfully we heard the runway had survived the earthquake.

I sensed for the first time a slight lifting of the heaviness in my heart as the thought of being home was starting to become a reality. But I was also aware that I still had a hell of a journey ahead of me. This was emphasised by what happened while we waited at Pheriche for our next helicopter taxi. Despite being told strictly not to take any more luggage than a personal rucksack, one person turned up at the helipad with three expedition duffle bags and an aggressive attitude. He demanded to get on board the next helicopter and was adamant that his insurance company had said it was all right for him to take all this stuff. This extra luggage meant that the two locals who were there, hoping to hitch a lift, would be left behind. Did he care about that? No. He did not care about that.

I was shocked and annoyed to see this kind of behaviour and though Tom and I tried reasoning with him, it didn't help. Unable to get back to their devastated families, the two humble locals slipped off away into the shadows. With little option the ground-man reluctantly gave in to this man's arrogant persistence. We crammed on board, sitting on top of his duffle bags in tense silence as the dangerously laden chopper eventually heaved itself off the ground and somehow wobbled through the thin air towards Lukla.

I had hoped my time in Lukla would be short; perhaps I would even get out the next day. But as soon as we landed at the airport, the chaos was apparent. I had noticed on the flight down that most buildings in the Khumbu valley had survived the quake. There didn't seem to be the huge swathes of wreckage I had expected to see, no more than a few collapsed buildings. This wasn't the case across the rest of the country, as the size and scale of the catastrophe was now clear. Nepal was in ruins, and it was estimated hundreds of thousands could be homeless. The final death count would be around nine thousand and Lukla had become a bottleneck for locals and foreigners who were desperately trying to get home as quickly as possible. Patience was a necessary virtue and now needed practising like never before.

I had not escaped completely unscathed. I couldn't stop the tremble that still pervaded my system. Even after countless bottles of Gurka beer, my food still shook on its way into my mouth. Lukla airport was crazily busy, the runway lined with cows, body-shaped tarpaulins, belongings and people. Hundreds of people. My dream of a swift exit had turned into the reality of being stuck here with everyone else. I shared a room with Henry Todd and one sleepless night turned into four or five, both of us in a similar state of emotional unrest. Neither had much to say but we were comfortable enough with each other to let the silence stand, disturbed only by the occasional fart.

During the endless wait for a confirmed flight, I did many laps of Lukla. On one such walk I bumped into Jason Laing, one of the heroic helicopter pilots who had now played a pivotal role in the aftermath of the two biggest disasters ever to hit the slopes of Everest. He was sitting on a wall next to a goat, wearing shades and drinking a coke. A casual hero in a crazy place. 'Thank you so much for all you've done for us,' I was pleased to be able to say. 'No worries!' was the modest response, delivered in his calm New Zealand accent. Because of the widespread devastation around Nepal, he told me the Government had commandeered all helicopters and were under strict instructions not to take any private bookings. This was to enable the massive relief efforts across Nepal, which was now the focus of international concern and explained why it was so difficult to get an aeroplane ticket. Jason's cool demeanour contrasted with my internal turmoil. I wondered how he could possibly deal with the amount of continued pressure he was under, day after day, while having to be technically proficient and clear in his decision making when life or death might be the consequence. Like his colleagues, he made no fuss about that, just quietly got on with the job.

I felt I had just about held myself together so far, but it wasn't sustainable. The finishing line kept moving further and further away and there was a limit to how much I could take before I broke down. This came to a head when I got an excited email from Julie. In all the chaos she had been misinformed that I was on a flight home when in fact I was still waiting in the crowds of the check-in hall. Having to write back with the news that I hadn't left was a tipping point for my emotions. I gave way to distress and frustration for the first time. I was also concerned about the impact this would all be having on Julie as she continued to recover from her treatment. I found myself on the verge of being overwhelmed by everything that had happened. I was wearing borrowed clothes; I hadn't slept properly for almost a week and my daily diet of Gurka beer and finger chips wasn't doing me much good either. Enough was enough. I needed to be home.

Eventually that day came. There was no excitement, just numb exhaustion as I stared blankly at the departures board, still juddering inside. Kathmandu was reeling in deep grief and widespread destruction. Teetering towers of tiny homes had fallen like dominoes on the fleeing residents beneath. The world heritage site of Durbar Square had been reduced to a pile of rubble and dust as had countless other temples and buildings. On the way to the airport for my connecting flight to London we passed a growing refugee camp, soon to become home to thousands who had lost everything and were desperate for help.

The airport itself was thronged with fresh-faced aid workers from all around the world all wearing their logos and brimming with good intention. I, on the other hand, was wandering around in someone else's pants, looking like a post-apocalyptic refugee. Once I was eventually on board my flight, I was shocked by my own state.

Somewhere there was joy at going home, but my body was still shaking as I tried to get comfortable in my seat. I put on a cheesy romcom to distract me but found myself completely unable to focus. This unnerved me almost to the point of panic. I couldn't follow the plot or even what the characters were saying. Nothing made sense at all. Minutes would pass and I would be unable to account for them. Where on earth was I? Then I was outside Heathrow hugging Sam and Lou, giving them the footage and sharing smiles of relief . . . I was in Glasgow coming though arrivals, seeing Julie through a cascade of tears . . . I was in the taxi dozing on her lap as she stroked my head . . . Then I was wide awake, fitfully spitting memories as we passed Loch Lomond. Somewhere beneath this crazy collage of fragmented time, I felt Julie's strength and love. She was there for me and, just as she had been so strong through her illness, I knew I also had to be strong. Finally, a week after the avalanche, I had Imogen and Jemima back in my arms and I was lying on my kitchen floor, surrounded with love and unable to move.

19

POST-TRAUMATIC STRESS

The weeks that followed were very tough. I was completely consumed by my experience. The same difficulties I'd had trying to watch that film on the flight had persisted into everyday life. When people spoke, their words weren't registering, as if they were speaking a different language. I was going over everything again and again, but not in any order. Reliving moments, speaking them out loud. Physically I was home, but mentally and emotionally I wasn't. I was in Nepal, wrapping the porters' bodies or shouting at the cameraman or struggling to breathe as my world caved in.

I was analysing my actions in the minutest detail, seemingly pulling myself apart before I could start putting myself back together again. Night-time was tough. Julie would be woken again and again as I screamed for helicopters, tossing and turning in sweat-soaked sheets. I was walking into Base Camp and becoming paralysed with fear as another avalanche broke free, burying me again just as I woke up.

My mind had become my enemy. If I tried to block the thoughts, it made things worse, so I let them come and experienced it all again on an unending replay. I'd read somewhere that the mind can go through a kind of filtering process as short-term memories become long-term ones. It didn't seem to be a smooth process. My conscience was working overtime, to make sure it was clear, sifting through my actions, on high alert for any feelings of regret or guilt that I could then use against myself as evidence in the ongoing trial in the court of Joe French's head. The inner witness I'd found on the glacier had put on a wig and become my judge. He was a tough one. Whereas my witness had been a silent presence, observing from somewhere else, my judge was the opposite. He was ruthless. Thank goodness I'd kept my camera in my bag. If I'd upset anybody by pressing record, I was sure I'd be sentenced to more suffering now. And what about those two dying porters, their eyes frozen open? What if their last view of this world had been me filming them die?

One morning, a few days into this relentless torment, I felt I had the strength to go for a walk. I was feeling a little better in myself and ready to have a brief outing. A short way up the road I bumped into a well-meaning neighbour. I smiled and said, 'Hi.' She looked me up and down, eyes wide.

'Oh my God, Joe, you look awful!' Her words cut through my thin veneer of stability and sent me reeling.

'Yeah I'm a bit rough,' I muttered, not looking at her.

'My goodness, I don't know where you start getting over something like that.' Then she went on her way, unaware of the damage she had done. Unintentionally she had destroyed me with those words. I gave up the walk, turned round and crawled back to bed, her words bouncing round my beleaguered brain.

A few days later I thought I'd try again. This time I jumped on my bike and headed towards the local trails. Once again, I had to abort the mission and retreat home. As I started to roll down the hill from our house, the wind picked up in my ears. It made me feel a little peculiar, but I carried on gaining speed regardless. After another couple of seconds, I could do nothing but slam on my brakes. My heart was racing, my mouth dry and a huge avalanche was chasing me down the road.

I skidded to a stop and jumped off my bike as the avalanche evaporated to nothing and I sat on the verge with my head in my hands. I was feeling that same judder from Nepal through my veins again. What was going on? The wind in my ears seemed to trigger some sort of audio hallucination, which then triggered an internal one. I couldn't see the avalanche coming with my eyes, but I could feel it coming through my nerves. Worried by what had just happened, I pushed my bike back home and made a cup of tea. This was perhaps a little more serious than I thought.

I arranged to see my GP and explained to him what had happened. He listened kindly and intently as I explained my experiences. 'Blimey, Joe,' was his appropriate response. He reassured me that the way I was feeling was a normal reaction to what I'd been through and I was likely to be suffering from Post-Traumatic Stress (PTS). Symptoms were common for the first month or so after the triggering trauma but should diminish with the passing of time. If this didn't happen, Post-Traumatic Stress Disorder (PTSD) could develop and symptoms would persist, and disrupt one's life going forward. PTSD can sometimes surface years after the event, in some cases without having PTS first, which was a useful, though daunting, piece of information to know.

Other than his knowledge and understanding, he couldn't offer anything but sleeping pills and a black and white photocopy of a PTSD fact sheet. It looked like it had been produced around the same time Wham! were topping the charts. I crumpled it into my pocket and thanked him as I left, choosing not to take the pills either. What I gained from that visit was reassurance that I wasn't going mad. I was just going through a process common to many, which was certainly a relief to know.

~

After a couple of weeks, the fight or flight response I seemed to be stuck in started to settle. Memories were no longer triggering fresh dumps of chemicals every time one popped into my head. The joy and relief of waking up one morning and realising I'd slept all night without waking was huge. As was the joy when Rob Smith arrived home from Nepal and came to see me. I'd last seen him leave for the Icefall a day or so before the earthquake. 'Hello, Joe French,' he greeted me in his usual way as he walked through my door, and I felt a definite lift in my mood. I sensed he knew where I was without saying a word and that knowing was exactly what I needed.

When the quake had struck, Rob was up at Camp 1 along with eighty or ninety or so other people. If we had felt cut off from the rest of the world that night, I can only imagine what it must have been like for those guys. Camp 1 teeters on top of the Icefall. The tents are precariously positioned around the many crevasses that dominate the area and although not an ideal setting, it is an important place for most people to spend a night as part of their acclimatisation. How terrifying it must have been to be so exposed when the quake struck. Their camp was hit by several waves of avalanche, mostly from the west shoulder, but thankfully not large enough to cause the same kind of damage as the previous year. Rob was aware there had been a major incident at Base Camp but was frustratingly powerless to help.

The route down through the Icefall was destroyed and it was out of the question to attempt to forge a fresh way. If down was out of the question, Rob wondered if going up to Camp 2 was maybe a wise move? Although it felt counter intuitive to be going up the mountain for safety, Camp 2 is a much more sheltered spot. As one of the more senior guides present, he had an agonising night of going through every option available, keeping everyone safe and wondering what had happened to all of us at Base Camp. As morning broke it wasn't too long before they heard that reassuring roar from down the valley and the decision was made for him. The helicopters taxied everyone down to BC in a couple of hours or so, completing another high-altitude rescue of epic proportions.

Rob had then stayed behind with Anthea, Guy and Scotty to help with the gigantic clean-up job at Adventure Consultants' camp. He then returned to Kathmandu just in time to be hit by another aftershock. At 7.3Mw on the scale, it was another terrible blow for Nepal and caused further loss of life and buildings. Many villages that had escaped the first quake were caught by this massive aftershock, bringing further devastation to a country already on its knees. One of the things that had stuck with Rob was meeting the Adventure Consultants Sherpa staff in Kathmandu. With shaved heads and freshly stitched scalp wounds, they were asking with concern if AC would be returning the following year. In addition to their injuries and shock, they were also deeply concerned about their livelihoods being taken away. At that moment Rob decided he would go back the following year. I respected him so much for that. The thought about whether I could do the same hadn't even crossed my mind.

As we sat and drank tea, Rob rummaged in his jacket pocket. 'Oh yeah,' he said casually, 'I found this buried deep in the snow.' In his shovel hand was a bent and bashed LaCie hard drive. It was those dodgy helicopter rushes I thought had been lost. They had survived and come back to haunt me.

'That's great,' I said, probably not sounding as delighted as he may have expected. Oh well, no escape from karma, I guess. Must remember the six Ps before going on a shoot next time next time: Prior Preparation Prevents Piss Poor Performance. I sent them off to Raw TV to be viewed and heard that they weren't that bad in the end. I must admit that the pressure of working in TV is very good at creating a whole lot of worry about nothing and I'm quite susceptible to this.

Rob left a great sense of relief in his wake. For the first time I had connected with someone who knew what I'd been through and that felt so important. I wasn't alone and that gave me strength. Despite being surrounded by all the love in the world, I had still felt somewhat isolated in those first couple of weeks. Rob had started building a bridge back to this world and soon I would be strong enough to take my first few steps.

20

RUNNING MAN 4: GOING BAREFOOT

2015

It wasn't a conscious decision to start running barefoot, it just happened naturally. The forest next door had provided a safe space I could walk through, knowing that I could be alone with my thoughts. Its drawback was how wet it was underfoot. I had three pairs of old trainers in rotation, always trying to get one dry enough to start the walk afresh. Complaints from Julie and the kids about the smell in our boot-room were well justified. Maybe I needed a different approach. Why not just take my shoes off?

I felt weird doing so, almost self-conscious as I undid my laces for the first time. Although my only witness was Ziggy the dog, I felt exposed and vulnerable as I lurched across the pebbles of our drive, hoping no one would see. But my, what a feeling it was to connect my sole to the soil inside the forest. What had I been missing all these years?

My tentative feet took a moment to adjust, as if re-registering old but familiar sensations. With a bit of toe wiggling and stretching, they began to unfurl into the soft blanket of moss underneath. I pushed my heels down hard and sank further into cushioned dampness, feeling a smile light my face at last. Slight twinges of happiness were detectable, just as real as the dominant darkness of my days, though still muted and muffled like the rest of the world outside of the forest.

I stood. Still. Rooted in a subtle exchange between moss and me. Then I collapsed to the ground and lay cradled and safe in a thick blanket of soft green. Then I was up, I was moving, completely oblivious to which direction I was moving in, I was just moving, my attention completely absorbed in each step. The snap of a stick. The slurp of a skid. The squelch of a swallowed sole. With each step, a different texture and sensation presented itself and the more I tuned into this, the more I tuned out of everything else. Moments turned to minutes, minutes turned to hours as I lost and found myself over and over again in this new world.

I started by following any deer trails I could find, clearing a few branches here and there to make space for me to run through on my next visit. My pace increasing with my enthusiasm, day after day I found myself in there again, each time trying a new trail or ways of linking two existing ones together. The faster I was running, the more I was having to concentrate and by consequence the more I became absorbed in my movement rather than my mind. I would know if my thoughts were getting the better of me again with a pang of pain from an absent-minded foot strike, bashing against an exposed root or pointy-up stick. I had to focus on each placement with maximum presence or I would soon know about it. This was what I needed, to focus on something that wasn't what I had just been through. My running was here and now and required me to be also.

During these explorations, I became increasingly obsessed with finding the most direct way to a particular place of peace I found, right in the heart of the forest. Through the trees one damp morning, I had spotted a clearing. It was an obvious direction to head in. After slowly picking my way through the shadows, I popped out of the trees and felt a smile spread across my face. A treasure lay before me. To the rest of the world, it would appear as a peat bog lochan, but to me it was a hidden jewel, shimmering with the power to heal and transform.

I would find my way to its jagged shoreline by a different route each day, and each day it was different in appearance and atmosphere. If a westerly wind was blowing, stormy black ripples charged across its surface. First you would hear gusts swooshing though the trees, then see them smash down and dance tempestuously over the water, before whipping them up into a spray that would needle my skin a few seconds later. On calm, clear days, it barely seemed possible that such turbulence could exist: the lochan was a mirror of forest green and sky blue, brimming with peace and reflection. Clouds would float across the stillness until they became fragmented by branches of birch, dipping and bobbing from the bank as if they were fishing with lines of lichen.

It was easy enough to get to this lochan from a variety of directions, but almost impossible to reach directly, without becoming disorientated or confused along the way. As the mental map in my mind grew with increasing information from my explorations, so had my urge to bring it all together. The purpose of my life, for a time, became finding the ultimate direct route to this hidden sanctuary. This process reminded me of being a child, climbing the wall of the ginnel in Sheffield to my mum's house instead of walking the long way round, or rock climbing directly through the hard section of a route, rather than avoiding it. I've always felt drawn to creating new lines through landscapes, as if I'm being carried along on the bristles of an artist's brush.

Each time I'd run into the forest's depths, I'd go a different way depending on how I was feeling. Sometimes I'd want to forge a new path, clear branches, and enjoy getting lost. Other days I'd want to follow trails I had already discovered and just be at one with the flow. Some days I would think I'd cracked it and had found the ultimate direct way, only to discover a better route the next time or that I couldn't remember which way I had gone the last. Always though, my direction would be towards this peaty jewel, and each time I got my first glimpse of its shimmer through the trees, I would experience the same thrill of satisfaction.

If I was paying enough attention, I could detect a subtle change of frequency as I emerged from the forest, not only of sound but also of feeling. On a calm day, the surface of the lochan would capture and amplify silence. The surrounding trees would hold it there in place. Within this space, waves of sounds could unwind and unravel into distinct layers, separating the hum of nature from the distant rumble of civilisation, broken only by the squawk of a jay or the splash-landing of a duck. It was easy to miss these subtleties when lost in my thoughts. Tuning in to this pristine *now* was the truest way to draw me out of my horrific *then*.

The lochan also had another power to help my struggling psyche – its temperature. Each time I reached its mossy, unde-fined shoreline I stripped down and gently eased myself in.

Dropping into its mysterious deep felt like trespassing at first. Even though I knew there were no crocodiles or monsters lurking beneath, my mind was very good at suggesting them as a possi-bility. There seemed to be a link between the depths of the water and the depths of my mind. I had to be brave while venturing into both. My goal wasn't to swim, it was just to stand. Stand as still as I could, no matter what the external conditions. Whether I was pelted with rain or bathed in sunshine, I would try to maintain my stillness. Both feet firmly in the soft peat below. Hands together in prayer fashion (to keep a pocket of warmth under my arm pits). And super-tuned to the sensations on my skin. Similar to the experience of running barefoot, this internal focus had the power to free me from my mind and deliver me straight back into my body.

On still days, my quickened heartbeat was enough to send concentric ripples out from my chest, across the mirrored sky to the furthest reaches of the lochan. Once I became more settled in the water and found a steady, deep rhythm to my breath, their frequency would change as my heart rate slowed.

I became witness again to my silent voice of panic. It could be telling me that it was too cold or crazy or that there was some previously undiscovered monster about to grab my legs. Whatever the reason, it was urging me to get out ASAP. But I would not give in. By maintaining stillness, I could let this narrative play out and focus instead on the feelings of ice and fire on my skin. The tingles of vibration fizzing through my veins. The vibrancy of the void within.

This void, I discovered, became brighter, deeper and more absorbing the more I focused fully on a steady rhythm of breath and the space between my eyes. No fancy breathing technique, just a series of deep long breaths in and out through my nose, until I pictured my whole system to be saturated with oxygen. The first few breaths always felt snatched, as my heart raced against the cold shock. But usually around breath four or five, I felt a tangible change, like a knot had been untied in my solar plexus. Once it had been undone, I instantly felt more relaxed and comfortable. I would then hold my breath and discovered that, with a little practice, I could transcend the feelings of cold for a short time. I could go on a little adventure through the swirl of my own consciousness. The beginning and end of this mediation was always turbulent, but somewhere in the middle there was a sweet spot where I could be somewhere else completely.

~

My run and dip in the lochan became a sacred daily routine. It gave me the structure and space I needed to recover, and I could feel how it was helping me to be me again. As the seasons changed and the first frosts of winter crept down from the mountain tops, it was harder to settle in my watery world. But I still would. Even when the snow and ice came. Each day I stripped down, feeling like a caveman preparing for his daily wash. Before I got in, I stood on the edge, frozen in a moment that could stretch for seconds or even minutes. It was a moment of transition. Once I flicked the switch of commitment, I became an observational passenger, witnessing myself heading towards a cold shock, hyper aware of everything in that moment, but reacting to nothing.

The two activities of barefoot running and cold-water immersion opened a space between me and my troubling thoughts. The horror of what happened gradually started to find a place where it could settle, while my attention was distracted and held elsewhere. Out of mind and into body. And the more I practised, the longer I could stay there.

21

EVEREST RESCUE

2016

'We've got a production coming up on Everest and we heard you're the man for the job.' My heart started racing and my hands were shaking. It was Dave Harrison in his office at betty TV in London. He had called as I was running up the Allt a' Mhuilinn in the direction of the CIC hut on Ben Nevis. 'Always interested to hear about Everest,' I panted and sat down on a stump. Winter had started to warm in the direction of Spring and both Julie and I were on the mend. Despite being shell-shocked by our experiences, we were doing all right and had a whole new appreciation for the mundane.

I smiled as Dave told me the subject of this new Discovery series: a remarkable group of helicopter pilots pushing their machines to the limits on Everest. 'I know them,' I told him proudly. 'Proper heroes that lot!' I would be embedded with Russell Brice's Himalayan Experience expedition and, as well as filming rescues at Base Camp, I might also have to climb with the team to Camp 2 and follow the action on the mountain.

Now here was a choice. The steady ground I had found over the past few months had been hard won. Though the ghosts were still there, my PTSD had died down. Could this seemingly great opportunity undo all the progress that I had made? Was my trauma best left gathering dust in a drawer or should I unlock it and see what happened? It was a huge decision and the more I thought about it, the more difficult it got. Procrastination became crippling. Over and over, I would weigh up the pros and cons. Dormant stress stirred back to the surface. The nightmares started again. I hadn't had any for months, but they started creeping back, taking form with the same old sequence. Walking into Base Camp and becoming unable to move as another avalanche swept down and engulfed me. I would wake in a pool of sweat next to a concerned looking Julie. Before I could give an answer, I needed to phone a friend.

Brian Tregaskis, or BT, as he is affectionately known to us, is head of the Belford Hospital in Fort William and Commander-in-Chief for all things medical in Lochaber Mountain Rescue Team. Most importantly he is a wonderful human being who has dedicated his whole life to making people well. I was, and am, a member of LMRT, but had not been on any rescues since Everest. I felt saturated by trauma and concerned about exposing myself again.

Brian, as ever, was happy to talk to me and I was summoned to his mad-professor-like office upstairs at the Belford. Under his whiteboard of scribbles and surrounded by a sea of interesting but complicated looking books, I told him everything as he sat nursing his cup of coffee. He looked directly at me only intermittently. This emotional distance was helpful. Hopefully he was forming the objective view that I needed. Then came my huge question at the end. 'Do you think I am well enough to go back and is it the right thing to do?'

His answer was incredibly helpful. It went something like this. 'Joe, you have a lot of friends out there who have no choice but to carry on. There will be a lot of folks out there who want to see you and whom you will want to see. It sounds to me that there is a part of you still in Nepal.' He paused for a moment before continuing. 'Maybe you have to go back before you can move forward. But I can't tell you if it's the right thing to do or not, that's up to you and your family to decide.' Brian's words shed light on my situation, and they took me away from the heaviness I was feeling. I cycled home extra quick.

It was hard to gauge how Julie felt about it all. She never created a fuss about anything. Even having cancer. She was always so supportive of my adventures in TV land, but the last year had been so incredibly challenging for both of us. How could I even be thinking about putting her and the kids through all this again? On the other hand, how could I not take this opportunity? Would I then be forever thinking *what if?* With each day of going round in circles, I tied myself up in bigger and bigger knots. With my mind caught in a loop, I had to trust my gut. What did I *feel* was the right thing to do, rather than what did I *think* was the right thing to do? My feeling was I should go.

'Brian suggested I may need to go back before I can go forwards,' I whispered to Julie after another difficult night. She snuggled into my chest and rubbed the sleepiness out of her eyes. I felt her nod in agreement. We lay in silence for a while. Imogen and Jemima were waking up next door, their happy voices discussing a tea party for their toys. Julie sat up and looked at me. 'We will be all right here, my love. I think you should go.'

I started this trip to Everest with a train journey from Brighton. I'd been visiting my younger brother Joshua and was on my way to London, to the office of betty TV, who were running the production. I felt so pumped full of excitement and nerves that I was wiggling in my chair. Listening to MC Yogi's *Elephant Power* and grinning wildly, I couldn't understand why my smiles to the other commuters were unreciprocated and met instead with puzzlement. Miserable bunch, I thought and carried on smiling with extra purpose as the world rushed by my window.

After Gatwick I grooved down the aisle to the toilet and, as the electric door slowly closed behind me, I got a shock. The perplexed looks weren't reflecting how the commuters were feeling, they were reflecting how I was looking. I had a huge smear of toothpaste on my chin and my shirt buttons were all misaligned by one. I cursed the booze from the night before and, as I left the toilet, I chose to go in the opposite direction and find another carriage to sit quietly in.

After a couple of weeks of prep in London, we were all set to go. The whole team felt positive and we were all desperate to get out there. For many it was their first taste of Nepal and I felt envious of them experiencing it for the first time. I was happy that John Griber, my friend and fellow summit cameraman from the 2014 expedition, would be my colleague again. Griber was a veteran of this environment and understood the politics we would have to navigate while filming up there. Laid back, with a dry sense of humour and bright blue eyes, he made everyone feel at ease around him. He'd summited Everest twice already and was also the first North American man to snowboard from 8000m on nearby Cho Oyu, the world's sixth highest mountain.

As our flight got nearer to landing in Kathmandu, I was aware that I was becoming increasingly subdued and finding it hard to concentrate on anything for more than a few seconds. I had contacted Chhongba and was delighted when he replied that he would come to meet me in Kathmandu, even though his village was miles away. My emotional state was heightened with this expectation as we came into land. I was gripping the arms of my chair with sweaty palms and breathing deeply. Was I ready for this?

Unfortunately, I was gripping the plastic of my chair for some time. We had to abort landing three times due to weather. I felt as if the gods were playing a game and controlling our toy plane as we circled the airport, banking between the angry anvils of electric downpours. Eventually the pilot gave up trying and we were informed over the tannoy that we had been diverted to Northern India because of the storm. This was excruciating news. I found it hard to join in with all the excited banter going on among my colleagues. I wasn't excited. I was anxious and withdrawn.

A few hours later we did eventually touch down in Kathmandu, but by this time there was no sign of Chhongba. In the blur of a stormy night, we made our way through the familiar streets and after an epic unload of gear, I collapsed into a big bed in the Hyatt Hotel and was immediately asleep.

The phoned beeped loudly. I didn't know where I was. 'Mr French, a Mr Chhongba is in reception to see you.' I rummaged through my bag for something to wear and bounded downstairs. Shirt buttons all out by one.

And there he was. Noble Chhongba in his bright orange jacket, armed with a huge grin and chains of flowers in his arms. 'Welcome back to Nepal, Joe!' he smiled and put flowers around my neck. I felt like a prince – then I burst into tears. We went to the hotel gardens and had breakfast together; there was plenty to catch up on.

Chhongba had some big blanks in his memory, so it was helpful to go through the events at the time of the avalanche. He could remember seeing the avalanche burst through the cloud but had no recollection of anything further until he came round in that hot, stuffy tent at IMG's makeshift hospital. He was walking with a limp from his injured hip, but other than his obvious sadness he was all right.

By dreadful misfortune, many of the buildings in Solo Khumbu that survived the first quake were destroyed by the 7.3Mw aftershock that hit a couple of weeks later. Just about all the Adventure Consultants Sherpa team needed help rebuilding their lives and houses, including Chhongba. When the builders got to work on his house in the village of Nunthala, they found a beehive behind his toilet bowl and got two litres of fresh honey out of it! His story made me laugh and cry. There was always a golden lining to be found with this wonderful man.

My trek back to Base Camp was an emotional one. I was lucky to have a sensitive crew around me and, as I followed the stories and characters from our expedition, I was also telling my story. Pete Campion, another shooting director, was trekking with us. He and Griber followed my wobbly journey back up the Khumbu. I just about kept it together for the walk in but knew that the climax was still to come – first eyes on Base Camp and the walls that surrounded it. I was both frightened and intrigued to see what effect it had on me. I had been wondering and dreaming about it for months.

A little after Gorak Shep, where the last tea houses are, the trail finds a ridge that runs alongside the glacier and winds its way to Base Camp. It was on one of its many crests that the moment happened.

I rounded a corner, and my body became instantaneously frozen and heavy, as if under the tremendous weight of an invisible force. I hit the dirt – not just crying but wailing. I got up and staggered a few more steps before the same thing happened again. The gravity of the situation was crushing. Step by step I walked into my nightmare. But there was no sign of any avalanche coming. Just a thickness to the thin air that I was almost having to push my way through – a sensation like sleep paralysis, but while wide awake. It was unnerving but I had no choice but to go with it. I was meeting my demons head on, and it wasn't pretty. I realised I must be having some sort of breakdown but was shocked at how over-whelming it was. A few more steps, then I'd collapse in tears again. Trekkers walked past with concerned faces. I tried to hold it together until they passed, before disintegrating again into another wave of tears. Griber was shocked by my state when he found me on the floor, but I could see what he was thinking – TV gold!

Between his questions, I managed to cry myself dry. A volcano of emotional lava must have been simmering inside for months. Maybe now it had erupted, I could start moving forward and leave all this emotion behind on the rocks. From my teary perch, I noticed our expedition members come into view. I was there to do a job and needed to get back to work. After a big hug from Griber, we split up and started filming our team as they made their way into Base Camp. I remember seeing Russell's annoyed face in my viewfinder. The first question he was asked by one of his new clients was, 'Why isn't the WiFi up and running yet?'

When all our team had arrived at Base Camp, I could finally put my camera down after a long, difficult day. I took myself off to my tent and collapsed. I couldn't even be bothered to take my boots off, so left my legs hanging through the door.

My hazy doze was broken by a slight rumble somewhere in the distance. I went from being semi-asleep to desperately clambering out of my tent in the space of a second. I emerged, all sweaty and panicked, only to find my friends chilling on the rocks outside.

'You all right, Joe?' Griber called over, his face in shadow under the peak of his beanie cap. An avalanche danced down a gully behind him.

'Erm yep, fine just . . .' There was no other way of putting it. 'Just a bit freaked out by that noise.'

Griber smiled. 'You'll have to get used to that, buddy!'

22

HIMALAYAN CRUMBLE

Having Russell Brice at the helm was perfect. Always cleanly shaven, with a wry smile and a gruff approach, he ran one of the most established, respected companies at Base Camp – Himalayan Experience. He was well known for reading conditions on the mountain correctly and getting his team up and down during the brief summit window safely. I think it's fair to say that other expeditions watched what Russ was doing, then followed his lead if they could. For that reason, his plans and preparations remained secret to all but a few trusted friends. This was to try to avoid his clients being caught up among the awful crowds and queuing in the 'death zone' of recent years.

This year the pressure on him was enormous, but he seemed to be coping with it well. After two years of Everest being closed for business, expectations were high for a successful season. Russ, along with his Sirdar, Phurba Tashi, would be leading the way with this. Another humble legend of the Khumbu, Phurba had summited Everest an incredible twenty-one times himself, but you would never have known it unless you asked him directly. Despite this year's pressure, safety would remain the pair's primary concern and Russell wasn't afraid of making tough decisions, as he had back in 2012.

That year, he made the controversial call to pull his clients off the mountain before they had made a summit attempt. His climbing Sherpa had been hit by heavy rock fall and found unstable ice in unusual places on the mountain. This rang alarm bells in Russell's head. Putting the safety of his clients first, he abandoned his expedition and brought everyone back to Base Camp. There were inevitably mixed feelings among his clients, since they had paid thousands for this opportunity. Russell was the only expedition to cancel that year, but his gut instinct was good.

2012 proved to be worse for fatalities than the 1996 *Into Thin Air* expedition that Jon Krakauer famously documented. Overcrowding on the mountain had reached critical levels and, after a record breaking 234 summited in one day, eleven people died on their way down. 547 summited in total that year and those infamous photos of the horrendous crowds in the death zone were the result of this. Yes, Russ could have got them to the top, but reaching the summit is only half the journey and when you may have to climb over the dying to get back down, you must wonder what you're doing up there in the first place.

Death is a high price for ambition. All who set out to climb Everest must think about that at some point. The 'conquering' of Everest has become an almost normalised pursuit. Maybe it is easy for people to overlook the fact that nowhere on this mountain is safe, not even Base Camp. Such a gamble needs to be considered seriously. You can learn with experience to read your route and visualise the moves and the difficulties that may await you on the way. With good judgment and the right equipment, you can minimise many risks, but you can never eliminate them completely.

This is particularly true on Everest, where the slopes are now teeming with folk who lack the ability to read the mountain for themselves. On top of that, there are catastrophic environmental processes going on – huge chunks of the mountain falling off or ice towers toppling. Your reward for making it through all of that could well be joining a multi-coloured conga line of fellow novices, gingerly queuing and plodding their way to the summit. The dream of Everest can be an absurd reality, but one that is deemed acceptable by the many willing to pay the price. Exactly what that price will be, is a mystery between you and your fate.

Russell set his expedition up a little differently to many. To avoid too many trips through the dangerous Icefall, he acclimatised by climbing nearby Labouche East Peak and spending a spectacular night on the summit. At 6119m, she's a big old beauty and it was a dream to be paid to climb it. Russell's lead guide was laid-back New Zealander Richie Hunter. He was there during the avalanche and shared that awful night in the Himex dome tent. It felt good to be climbing with him and, even though we didn't speak about it much, we were immediately bonded through our shared experience.

The climbing wasn't technically difficult, but there was some complicated route finding through broken slabs and cliffs to begin with, then a steady snow plod to the summit. It felt great to be doing what I do best, buzzing around the group, strong and confident on the ground as I captured it all. The lack of ice and vast areas of exposed rock on display made me wonder though: any snow and ice that was there seemed to be disappearing in front of our eyes. This was made more obvious as I filmed Richie battling to get his ice screws into rotten honeycombs, while trying to fix our ropes. It took a few attempts to find any ice strong enough for his screws to bite into and I could see the fun he was having as I kept the camera rolling. I could also under-stand his hesitation to speculate on the conditions when I asked him about the effect the warming climate would have on the mountains.

I had noticed a definite change at Base Camp. In 2014 there was only solid glacier to camp on. Now, three years later, there was a bright river flowing right through camp, creating marvellous ice sculptures in its wake. It is true that this river does start to flow every year, but usually it is held frozen until the climbing season is over and Base Camp is being packed up for the summer monsoon. This year you had to wade through it before any climbing could begin.

Camping on the summit of Labouche East was both the highest and most spectacular night I'd ever had. I was so excited about the view at sunrise that I gave myself a headache. I kept peeking out of my tent to see if the stars and galaxies on display were becoming any less bright. I think my enthusiasm may have annoyed Griber, who was trying to sleep. I kept kicking him. Try as I might, I just couldn't settle down. I wanted to get a time-lapse of the sunrise, so I lay with my batteries in my armpits to keep them warm and ready, full of charge. Maybe they were charging me up as well.

Eventually the dark started to dissolve, and I was out of my tent quick, covering Griber in a shower of ice. He grunted at me as I crawled out and breathed in the full glory of my first Himalayan summit sunrise.

Great waves of the world's highest peaks flowed in every direction, before falling away towards the Tibetan plateau to the north. The silence seemed to buzz with a frequency that I don't think was tinnitus. I needed a few moments to compose myself to avoid another headache. Hundreds of miles away the snow was starting to turn pink in the east and it was time to set my camera up. With numb fingers and toes, I fumbled the tripod level and pressed the red button. Slivers of light soon turned to slices, and the slopes became illuminated with peach and pink and orange.

From my throne on the top of the world I was a king that morning. Once the sun hit the boulders at Lobuche on the valley floor, Andy Tyson joined me. Together we sat for a while, watching the clouds twist and twirl round the summits, before spiralling off through thin air to dissolve into space.

23

TAXI FOR ONE

I shed a tear on seeing Rachel Tullet and Greg Vernovage again. We were at IMG's Puja ceremony, in an emotional, celebratory atmosphere. Rachel was back as Base Camp manager for Jagged Globe, hoping to get the chance to venture onto the mountain herself. I hadn't known how badly her leg had been injured when the avalanche hit. Only when she had treated all the casualties, did she stop and stitch herself up. She played this down and instead focused on the combined efforts of everyone to get us through that awful day. 'Thank you for not filming us,' she said after we had chatted for a while. Greg agreed. I was incredibly pleased and grateful to hear those words.

The intensity of my stress then among so much trauma had left me frozen. It was more than a decision whether to film or help, it was a question of who I was. If I hadn't had a camera, I would have just got on and helped, as everyone else did. But for me, helping was racked with guilt. Even though I knew it was the right thing to do, I was constantly stressing. I'd just lived through the biggest disaster ever to hit Everest and I kept my filming to a minimum. What kind of producer was I?

I'd come into the expedition already stressed by what we'd been through with Julie's cancer and the previous year. Andy Tyson's death was devastating, and the evacuation of Sam and Lou had put a whole lot more pressure on my shoulders. Then the

163

avalanche and its aftermath. Perhaps there was only so much I could take before it all became overwhelming, and only possible to deal with later, in the form of PTS or PTSD. Maybe going to Everest ER to look for supplies had been a tipping point. Had my brain blown a fuse? Was my experience of PTSD a mental injury rather than an illness? In the same way that lifting heavy objects repeatedly will eventually injure your body, could prolonged exposure to high levels of stress have injured my mind? I hadn't just been reliving moments as I processed them, I'd been experiencing them again as a physical reality.

Rachel and Greg saying thanks for not filming them felt instantly healing. They were words that I'd needed to hear. If I'd listened to that other voice, the one that was encouraging me to film, how would I be feeling now?

From first to last light, the sky was full of helicopters. Most days there would be at least twenty, maybe thirty landings at the five or so makeshift sites around Base Camp. Some would be rescuing, some delivering supplies, some dropping off tourists who would wander around a bit, then quickly leave before the altitude started to kill them. If the weather changed and the chopper couldn't fly, it might just do that. One tonne of rope and fixing equipment was even flown up to Camp 1 for the first time that year, saving between 80 or 90 Sherpa journeys through the Icefall. Everest Base camp wasn't a place of tranquillity, it was a high-altitude depot.

There was a rumour that one of the expedition companies had links with a helicopter company and had a clever way of maximising profits. After flooding the mountain with inexperienced mountaineers on cut-price expeditions, knowing full well that they were likely to get into bother, they would then send their own helicopters in to rescue them. They could then charge the clients' insurance companies top dollar for the privilege and make a profit at both ends of the deal.

One morning, I was alerted to a real-time rescue happening at Camp 1. The helicopter came into land, and I was poised and ready to capture the poor injured soul as he was carried off. When the doors opened, a muscular man in a big yellow jacket jumped out and walked off towards his tent. I waited for the injured man to appear and wondered why the man in yellow had left without helping him out. Then, the door closed, the chopper flew off and that was that. I checked with the groundman if I had got the right helicopter. He confirmed with me that the man in yellow was indeed the injured man requiring rescue.

I could still just about see him wandering across the ice, so ran after him. Out of breath and confused, I asked him what had happened and if I could film him to explain his story. He was absolutely delighted by this prospect, so we settled down in his tent and got rolling.

He was a rich Saudi who had felt exhausted up at Camp 1. The Icefall had freaked him out so much he didn't want to go back through it. He called for the helicopter like calling for a taxi and he could see absolutely nothing wrong in doing so. I was exasperated, but kept my professional head on, filmed some cutaways and left him to his luxuries. As far as he was concerned it was a service that was on offer and he had the money to pay for it, so why not?

The ongoing commercialisation of Everest, now with a flying taxis service, had brought a new type of consumer to the slopes, hoping to buy the experience of Everest without having to suffer its hardships. Was this place becoming the Disneyland of mountaineering and the helicopters its rollercoaster rides?

The anniversary of the earthquake was the 25th April. On that day a minute's silence descended across Base Camp as most expeditions marked this sad milestone with a reflective pause for thought. We lit candles for everyone who had died and stuck them in an upturned egg box. The flames flicked and fizzed as we stood arm in arm, watching these tiny flames struggle in the thin air. Behind us the wall of Pumori and the path of the avalanche loomed large. I knelt to blow the candles out and my composure left me. I stayed crouched on the ground, sobbing.

It felt good to let go among my new friends. Submitting and letting this wave of tears carry me as far as it needed to go was empowering. It wasn't on the scale that I had experienced when I saw Base Camp for the first time but was enough to leave me feeling exhausted afterwards. Even those who weren't present in 2015 were visibly upset – a scene that must have been repeating itself all over Base Camp. After things settled down and the whisky came out, Griber and I stumbled up to Ground Zero and met with Rob Smith and Anthea Fisher. They were perched on the boulders, among the mangled metal and random relics left behind in the moraine. The glacier was already moving on, slowly consuming what remained of the tragedy into itself. It was taking me a little longer.

Russ had spotted an early summit window that seemed to have been missed by most of the other expeditions, many of whom had left Base Camp and were replenishing themselves on thicker air, further down the valley. It was decided that Griber would follow and film the team. As we didn't have summit permits, the plan was to go as far as the Lhotse Face, then wait at Camp 2 for their (hopefully) triumphant return. As it turns out, Griber didn't have to wait at all. The team left and were back down at Base Camp after only a couple days. There had been delays, mostly caused by weather, to the fixing of the ropes on the mountain higher up, which made it impossible to go for an early summit.

Instead, they retreated to Base Camp to rest and give the fixing team time to get the job done. I knew that a serious chat was on the cards for Griber and me. Upon leaving I had told Julie that I wouldn't be climbing, but now it seemed I might have to re-think that plan. On the one hand I was petrified by the prospect. I had seen first-hand how dangerous it was up there and, after all my family had been through, how could I justify the extra risk that climbing would entail? On the other hand, Griber also had a family. Was it fair to ask him to go through the Icefall again on their next attempt, just because I was too scared?

I was consumed by this conundrum for some time. I took myself off into the glacier to crystallise my thoughts. Leftfield's *Release the Pressure* was booming in my headphones, and I found myself starting to dance, first self-consciously, but as no one could see me but the gods on the summits, I started to carve some proper shapes. Throwing my hands up and pumping the sky, I felt I was dancing with my demons face to face. I could see the bodies soaring underneath the helicopters. I could feel the avalanche swallowing me again. I looked up to the summits and felt the bass line kick in. This was me. This was now. I had to climb.

24

VALLEY OF SILENCE

Our team was a well-bonded, international bunch: Tracee Metcalfe, a medic from Colorado; Andreas Friedrich, a flight captain from Germany; Jaco Ottink, a seven summiteer from the Netherlands; Takayasu Semba, a businessman and climber from Japan and Greg Paul, a climber and businessman from Utah. It had already proved too much for Hardeep Rehsi from the UK who couldn't convince Russell that he was strong or quick enough for the rigours of the mountain higher up.

I had become very fond of Greg Paul through the time we had spent together on this trip. His story was an inspiration. He was a man of strong Mormon faith and, at sixty-one, the oldest member of our team. If successful, he would become the first American man to summit after two knee replacements. I had first spotted him sitting in the corner of a guest house, wearing a Pink Floyd T-shirt. He was enjoying reading a climbing article and his manner was mellow and friendly. He was co-founder of Momentum Climbing Walls, a chain of indoor walls born out of Utah, and I was immediately drawn to him.

Greg's youth had been spent doing wild ski tricks and jumps off roofs which had knackered his knees, but not his enthusiasm for adventure. He'd attempted Everest in 2012, but Russ had called the expedition off. He tried again in 2014 but once again left in sad circumstances after the Icefall avalanche. During these trips Greg had become good friends with Ngawang Tenzing Sherpa, his climbing Sherpa from Phortse, and kept in regular contact with him. Greg had spent time helping him with his English skills online and, after the Earthquake, had helped financially as his family went about the process of rebuilding their home and life. The bond between them was clear. If Greg was going to get to the top, Ngawang was the man to get him there. 'Third time's a charm, or three strikes and you're out!'

The crunch of our steps was amplified in the stillness of night. I couldn't spot any other groups setting off and that felt exciting. Wise Russell was playing his game of Everest Chess and moving his pieces into position while everyone else was sleeping. Our crunches at times turned to splashes as we waded in and out of the sparking river that took us to the gates of the guardian of Everest, the Khumbu Icefall.

After three years of looking up at it from my tent I was finally in it, and it felt terrifying. Richie gave us one last pep-talk as we put on our crampons. The crux of his words was: 'Once inside you gotta keep moving till we are out the other end,' followed by, 'We want to be through the worst before the sun comes up and things start to melt.'

No one wanted to say much to my camera, but they didn't need to as the look in everyone's eyes said it all. We had a sense of the strange frozen shapes that loomed around us but couldn't see in any detail the route that lay ahead. Solemnly, we clipped into the start of the fixed rope that led from here to the summit and shuffled off into this most other-worldly of worlds.

I scampered around as usual, getting in front and to the side of the group to give a variety of shots for the edit. The rope serves as a route finder, weaving its way around and over the many obstacles one has to cross. To get round everyone I was having to unclip and move quickly, otherwise my shots would all have been of everyone's bums. It was risky, but I felt confident enough to do so and my climbing skills helped a lot. While others were battling with their jumars to get up the short walls of ice, I could solo past them with my camera in one hand, getting some good shots on the way. Great gargoyles of ice were watching and waiting above us, seemingly alive in the darting beams of our torchlight. Alarming groans and cracks punctuated our silent scratching, serving as warnings that this was no place for humans to be.

Our first major obstacle was a large crevasse. To cross it, we had to teeter across two aluminium ladders. They had been lashed together in the middle with cheap rope and secured to surrounding ice with more cheap rope and wobbly ice screws. It's a tricky process, as you need to get the tips of your crampons right on the rungs otherwise your foot can disappear. You are clipped in with a cow's tail (small length of rope on your harness) to a safety rope to prevent you being swallowed alive. This rope didn't help stability but, as it ran along both sides of the crevasse, you could pull it tight towards your body with both hands and give yourself some sort of a handrail to help you across.

This first crevasse turned into many, and we were boosted by our great progress. That was until we were brought to a halt when Greg Paul went very quiet and disappeared into the dark. A little investigation found him crouching beneath a particularly mean looking ice tower with the contents of his rucksack emptied onto the ice. What was he doing?

His head-torch had failed, and he was searching for his spare batteries somewhere deep in his bag. 'I know they're in here somewhere,' he confessed as we all waited nervously underneath an imposing tower of ice. If it wasn't so dangerous, the whole scene would have been quite humorous, with Richie playing the exasperated teacher standing over his embarrassed student as he continued his panicked rummaging.

'Why didn't you put fresh ones in before we set off?' was Richie's obvious question.

'Err . . .' There was a somewhat inclusive answer. It sounded like an excuse for missing homework. Eddie the Yeti, the cuddly toy strapped to the side of Greg's bag, stared at us with its goggly eyes and cheery grin throughout.

It wasn't the first time Greg had had a comical mishap in this most serious of places. On a previous expedition he had lost so much weight by the time he made his return journey; he was struggling to keep his trousers up. These trousers eventually gave way under the weight of his harness, just as he was climbing down a ladder. He had no choice but to continue to the bottom of the ladder while exposing himself to the world – both hands were obviously needed for the task at hand. As he reached the ladders end, he was shocked to find nothing but a gaping crevasse and a whole lot of space waiting for him. It then dawned on him that he must have gone off route and was in fact climbing down the wrong ladder from an abandoned route. He had no choice but to climb back up with trousers round his ankles before he could sort himself out. Lucky he realised the error of his ways, otherwise the legend of Greg Paul would have had an unfortunate ending.

Our next obstacle was an 80ft vertical ice cliff that had been rigged with five ladders, lashed top to tail. It didn't just wobble, it heaved and squealed as my shaky foot gingerly found its way up each rung. Below I could hear a Sherpa repeating the mantra *Om mani padme hum* under his breath as I sketched my way up. I didn't know if it was for his benefit or mine. Thank goodness it was a quiet morning. On a busier day we could find ourselves part of a dangerous bottleneck as crowds of climbers waited for their turn, before snaking their way up one by one.

We were through the worst of it by the time we were able to switch our head-torches off. The dawn felt almost mystical, heightened I think by the four hours or so of fearsome exercise we had just lived through. A spectacular Dali-esque land of ice sculptures and tunnels to the underworld revealed themselves. Until now they had just been dark shadows lurking all around, menacing in their magnitude, but remaining mysterious and hidden. Now, as we stood speechless in the fizzing half-light, looking back at our improbable route, they somehow didn't seem so fearsome. These sentiments were abruptly ended by a huge crack and groan close by. We quickly scrambled on our way again, resisting any urge to be seduced by the beauty of our surroundings.

The last obstacle to overcome was the giant head wall of the Icefall. It's created as the glacier spills out of the Western Cmn and flows at a steeper angle to Base Camp below. It stands 30m or so high, and despite being vertical, it is easily climbable with your jumar and a good kicking technique. The excitement of my escape was enough to get me up there double quick and bank the final shots of my sequence – a triumphant Greg as he emerged from the belly of the beast. With one final heave I popped out of the top of the Icefall and was treated to a sight beyond beauty, the great Valley of Silence. I was in the Western Cmn. I had no time to take it all in, as Greg Paul was hot on my heals. I unclipped from the rope, ran a few extra steps then turned to frame my shot. The crystalline peaks of Pumori and Lingtrin in the immediate background, the sun rising over the vast Himalayas behind – what a shot it would be! I crouched down to steady myself and my elation turned to horror.

I looked through my viewfinder to discover everything was black. There was nothing to be seen at all. *Please tell me this isn't happening*! I could feel my face throbbing as I quickly tried to figure out what the problem could be. Turned it off and on again. Still nothing. Was it battery? No. Was it the lens cover? No. Was it the settings? No. Please dear God, what was it?

As I frantically turned the camera round and round, the lens wobbled then fell off into the snow. The adapter I was using to enable the lenses had come loose, probably as I'd smashed my way up that final wall. Luckily the lens had somehow stayed on. Quickly fixing it all back together, I pressed the red button just as Greg's head popped into frame like some kind of high-altitude whack-a-mole. I held the shot as he staggered towards the rest of the group, complete with cuddly toy at his shoulder. He looked like a cross between Clint Eastwood and Mr Bean and was glowing with relief. And so was I. I stood up, took a few steps back to get my wide shot, and my foot nearly went straight into a crevasse that, in my haste, I hadn't noticed was just behind me.

The Western Cmn is a hanging valley and hidden kingdom, surrounded by colossal, shimmering walls of ice. Mallory had first spotted this as a possible route to the summit in 1922 but dismissed it as he thought the Icefall looked impenetrable.

Everest is to the left, Nuptse to the right and Lhotse looms at the head of the valley where the Khumbu glacier starts its epic journey. It is known as the 'Valley of Silence' for good reason. The wave of serenity that hits you is almost audible. Danger persists, but the width of the valley, which at some points is a good kilometre wide, gives you some feeling of safety. The route ahead winds through a series of gigantic crevasses around Camp 1, before becoming more central and heading up the middle of the glacier, thankfully further away from those looming seracs. The team had already spent a night at Camp 1 on their previous rotation, so we carried on straight to Camp 2 at 6500m. I gave myself a rest from filming and slipped into my imagination as I wandered between crevasses and stared up at the heavens.

I felt the delight of Hillary and Tenzing when they first entered this sanctuary, realising that perhaps their dream could come true. I pictured Chris Bonington spotting his Southwest Face route and becoming determined to climb Everest *The Hard Way*. I thought of Ueli Steck, exploring the slopes of Nuptse, and slipping to his death. Countless dreams and tragedies witnessed from above by these three stoic giants. Their magnetic force pulling people from all walks of life and all over the globe onto their vast slopes. I could feel that power pulsing through me. How magnificent it was to be here. At least in that moment.

I spotted Camp 2 way before I reached it. As the sun had risen, so had the temperature and before long my daydreams were replaced by the numb sensation of being baked like a bean. The gigantic walls of ice rising either side were helping to turn the Western Cmn into a huge high-altitude convection oven and, under my many layers of clothing, I could feel myself shrivelling. The temperature range inside the Western Cmn is remarkable. It is often between thirty and forty degrees centigrade during the day but can rapidly drop to below freezing if the sun is obscured and the winds pick up. At night, minus twenty is common. I found it was best to keep myself fully clad as the combination of thin air and UV radiation felt enough to melt my skin.

The multi-coloured tents of Camp 2 were shimmering like a mirage in a silver desert. For hour after hour, they didn't seem to be getting any closer. I had planned to film our arrival at camp, but this was out of the question. I'd let the group get ahead as I dawdled and day-dreamed, and now there was no way I could catch them up. Even though the angle was gentle, each step required tremendous effort. I would manage four or five before needing to rest in the snow. I wondered if anyone had ever tried to fry an egg on the ice. By the time I eventually reached camp, I was utterly closed to the beauty of my surroundings. All I could do was crawl into my yellow canvas oven and roast myself dry, unable to do anything but groan.

25

GODS & GHOSTS AT
THE ROOF OF THE WORLD

At the head of the Western Cmn, a vast Bergschrund (large crevasse) opens up beneath the Lhotse Face. It's the point at which the Khumbu glacier starts peeling away, towards Base Camp below. As we approached, Richie and I stopped dead in our tracks. I glanced up at the Lhotse Face, which was now just in front of us, and was startled to see what looked like a Nepalese figure sitting upright and tobogganing with incredible speed down the ice, before disappearing silently into the Bergschrund.

'Did you see that?!' I asked Richie over the chit-chat of the rest of the group, who were oblivious to the sight. Richie nodded with a look of disbelief, confirming he had indeed seen the same thing. The next hour or so was spent searching all around the Berg-schrund. So convinced we had seen somebody, we even rigged a rope up and had a good look inside its depths for any signs or clues as to what we had witnessed but found nothing. No tracks, no noise, no blood, no nothing.

We radioed round the camps to see if anyone had been reported missing, but no one had. Were we going mad? It certainly wasn't a figment of our imagination, but with nothing to go on and a team waiting to get going again, we had no choice but to continue our climb. It was suggested that perhaps it was a falling rucksack, which although possible, didn't satisfy me as an explanation. Although it is very common for the mind to play tricks at altitude, whatever Richie and I saw that day will remain a mystery, a vision I can still see clearly in my mind's eye.

This weirdness reminded me of an incident involving Andrew Greig at ABC on the Northeast Ridge of Everest during his 1985 expedition. He wrote about it in his book *Kingdoms of Experience.* For a good hour or so he, along with Mal and Liz Duff, had sat and watched a man in a red wind-suit moving up the ridge between 7090m and Camp 3. The figure could be seen clearly silhouetted, both with binoculars and the naked eye, climbing well. They thought it must be Sandy Allan, one of the lead climbers, carrying a load to Camp 3 from Camp 2, where he had spent the night. That was until Sandy appeared in the mess tent behind them. 'What are you doing here?' they asked, shocked to see him arrive. Sandy was taken aback. He'd had a rough night, then descended, not even making it up to 7090m. They went back outside to see if the man in red was still there, but he had vanished. The only other climbers on the hill were well above Camp 3 already. Who on Earth had they been watching? And was he even of this Earth?

Earlier in the expedition, Jon Tinker, another lead climber, had found a snow cave used by Chris Bonington's expedition three years previously. Inside he found various items of clothing, including a red wind-suit belonging to Pete Boardman, who, along with Joe Tasker had sadly disappeared somewhere on the ridge, never to return.

The explanation Andrew came up with blew my mind. He didn't believe it was a ghost, more a visual echo or recording. He felt he was watching an event that had happened there three years earlier and had somehow become imprinted on the ridge itself. A glitch in the space time continuum? A window into a different dimension? Whatever it was, Andrew, Mal and Liz were of sound mind during this sighting. For an hour they had sat and watched a man who wasn't there.

Not long after seeing the Nepalese figure seemingly disappear into the Bergschrund, it was time to say farewell to my expedition as they started their slow journey up the Lhotse Face to Camp 3. I finished my sequence by filming six shimmering silhouettes shuffling silently up the ice. Beautiful as the scene was, I was struggling to frame up a shot because of the extreme glare and brightness. In the end, not wanting to fry my eyeballs by taking my glasses off, I just set the exposure and focus and pointed the camera in their general direction, hoping for the best. I wondered how I would have managed to find a flying Joby Ogwyn soaring through the air at 200km/h. I couldn't even see these guys. 'Sorry, New York,' I imagined myself confessing, 'It's too bright, I think I've lost him.'

The next couple of days got progressively harder. I struggled with the altitude and had nothing else to do or think about other than that. There were only two of us left at camp, the cook who had a hacking cough and gastric problems, and me. Sleep came in small bursts and became progressively elusive. Cheyne–Stokes respiration started to develop, which meant each time I nodded off, I would wake suddenly gasping for air as if an elephant was sitting on my chest. I became obsessed with checking my oxygen level, even though it just made me feel worse. At its lowest it was down to a spectacular 56 percent, which at sea level would have had me in intensive care. My resting heart rate was about 120bpm, and I felt as if I was slowly dying.

I took some Diamox, a drug used to aid acclimatisation, to see if that would help me to feel better, but instead it made me feel worse. All my limbs started to tingle with pins and needles, and

I started peeing constantly, even though I was already dehydrated. The luxury of supplementary oxygen would have certainly helped me out.

Meanwhile, Greg was also having a tough time up at Camp 3. He was sharing a tent with Andreas Friedrich, a spiritual 54-year-old flight captain from Germany, with whom I had also got along very well during the expedition so far. I'd interviewed him during the trek in, after which he'd rummaged around in his pocket to produce some 'precious good stuff' for me. Intrigued and unsure what to expect, I watched as out came a well-shrivelled nub of ginger. 'Chew this,' he said with a grin, 'it has very healing properties!' I accepted his kind gesture and we'd been friends ever since.

Andreas took it upon himself to look after Greg at Camp 3. He melted snow to boil the water, did the cooking and Greg, frustrated at himself for not being able to do more, could do nothing but try to rest and recover. The following night at Camp 4 on the South Col, Greg was feeling slightly better and, as he arrived before Andreas, returned the favour by getting the tea made, ready for his German friend's arrival. The pair squeezed into their two-man tent and shared an uncomfortable few hours. They were perfectly placed for the summit window that seemed to be opening out before them, but all was not well.

The pair were anxious, exhausted, and having problems sorting their gear out. With the clock ticking down to their departure in just four hours, they were getting more and more frustrated at their lack of progress towards rest. At the point of almost being overwhelmed, Greg needed help. As a man of strong Mormon faith, he reached out for God. 'Andreas,' he said from his sweaty, disorganised half of the tent, 'can we just stop and say a prayer?' Andreas, despite being agnostic, agreed. They stopped their fumbling and sat huddled together, two men in a fragile state, on the verge of what could be both the biggest and the last day of their lives, tuning into the frequency of faith to guide them through.

This may have helped their minds and souls, but not Greg's personal admin situation. At around 12:30am, it was time to set off for the summit, but unfortunately the day didn't start too smoothly for the man from Utah.

I was dozing on and off in my sleeping bag, with the radio tuned in, listening in a dreamy haze to things getting under way up at Camp 4. The mountain was still relatively quiet, conditions were good and Russell's tactics of getting into position early seemed to be paying off. But Greg couldn't find his glove liners, and, because of his knees, he found it a challenge to get any gear on inside the confines of the two-man tent. It was easier to wait for Andreas to get out and give him room to move around. But then he couldn't get his crampons to fit and for the life of him couldn't figure out why.

This frustrated Russ, who was monitoring progress back at Base Camp. Like a caring but scolding father figure, Russ was again on Greg's back. He believed in his chances of reaching the summit, but at times was flabbergasted by his somewhat individual style of self-organisation. Even the thought of Russ's frowning face was enough to make Greg feel more flustered than he already was. He didn't want to let Russell down and despite it being hard to hear at times, appreciated all the tough love he had showed him.

Greg had left his boots outside in the vestibule overnight, which was a mistake. In all the early morning commotion and nerves, he had failed to see that the sole had become completely iced up, which was why his crampons no longer fitted. Thankfully Ngawang, Greg's minder-in-chief, was keeping a close eye on him. He bounded over in his full Apache kit, spotted the problem, and chopped the ice off with his axe. Finally, this meant Greg was ready, but now a good twenty minutes behind the rest of the group. His confidence had already taken a hammering, but Ngawang set off at a good pace and Greg followed on in his footsteps. Soon the pair were moving well together, and summit day was under way. There were only about thirty-five other people on the mountain that day and, as they climbed over the 8000m mark, they were going well enough to start overtaking some of those folk on the fixed lines.

As dawn broke, most of the Himex team had just about reached the South Summit, a few hundred metres from the main summit. Then things started to get a little spicy. An unsuspected storm blew in. Success hung in the balance. Visibility was down to 40ft and strong icy winds of minus 35° were battering hard against them, even causing Tracee Metcalfe's oxygen mask to freeze up and work only intermittently.

In this howling wind, it was hard to make out the radio chat between Richie and Russ. Richie was at the South Summit. Russ was watching with a telescope from Base Camp below. A three-way discussion was underway between the two of them and Phurba as to whether enough was enough and it was time to turn around. The Sherpa seemed happy to continue, but it was clear that the team were treading a very thin line between dreams and disaster. If the weather deteriorated further, Russ would have to pull the plug, despite their being so tantalisingly close to the summit. However, if the storm dissipated, they were perfectly placed to achieve their dreams of a lifetime. There was tremendous pressure on Russ. Not only did he have a camera in his face the whole time, but he also had plenty of visitors from other camps turning up and asking questions.

From Russ's position below, it looked like the storm was local to the summit. In fact, despite it being a white-out, Russ could make out individual figures of his team moving through the cloud at the South Summit with his telescope, indicating that the cloud was thin. This, along with the forecast that winds would drop before picking up again, gave him confidence to suggest they wait it out for a short while to see if conditions improved. Though this was possible, it was more of a risk than he would usually prefer to take, especially when other expeditions had already made the decision to turn around. The Himex team didn't want to hang around for too long. Standing still in the death zone gave the grim reaper a very good chance of catching up.

Meanwhile, Greg Paul was still stomping up the slopes with his new knees like a man possessed. At the South Summit he and Ngawang caught up with the rest of the team. Now feeling psyched up and strong, the pair didn't want to stop moving. Sensing that the plug may just be about to be pulled, Ngawang quickly changed Greg's oxygen bottle and pointed upwards. 'We go!' he said and that was that. They were off.

I was now fully awake and glued to the radio 'Go Greg!' I shouted, imagining Eddie the Yeti all iced up, hanging off his bag as he triumphantly strode into the storm. This was indeed Greg's moment – was it to be third times a charm or three strikes and you're out? I could barely take the suspense. I buried myself further into my bag, hoping that they would be okay as silence descended across the airwaves.

Somewhere above, the pair, along with Eddie the Yeti, fought their way along the corniced ridge with no problems. Soon the famous landmark of the Hillary Step came into view. The usual rocky cliff that forms this crux step was completely buried in snow, nothing more than a ramp. One half of it had avalanched into Tibet, leaving a smooth, relatively safe fracture line for them to follow up the mountain side. At the top of this Greg had a moment of realisation. He and Ngawang were the only people up there. Probably the highest people in the world at that moment. What a feeling! The storm still raged, but Greg liked storms and, as all seemed okay, there was no immediate reason to stop the ever-upwards plod towards the top. And so, they continued.

Around two hundred feet from the summit, the fixed lines ended abruptly. It was impossible to tell the snow from the sky, but Ngawang on his home mountain was keen and confident. 'Summit!' he shouted through the wind, indicating that they should keep climbing. Greg nervously followed, completely trusting Ngawang's judgement, but also completely reliant on him should things go wrong.

After what seemed like an age, the radio roared back into life. It was 8am. Greg's voice was trembling with excited exhaustion, barely audible through the crackles and wind. 'We've made it!' He proudly proclaimed, 'We're on the summit!' I whooped with delight as I heard this come through, sending my breakfast of cheese and chive Pringles spilling out all over my tent.

Back at Base Camp, Russ was also delighted, though surprised that it was Greg that had made it there first, especially after the bad start he had made that morning. But now they were standing on the summit prayer flags, which were under a large mound of snow. Later Greg joked they'd had to climb a few feet higher than Hillary and Tenzing to make it to the top. One by one, the rest of the team followed in Ngawang's and Greg's footprints and by the end of the morning, everyone in Himex's 2016 expedition had made it to the top, the first fully commercial team of the season to do so. Everest was open for business once more.

For a moment I wished I was there too, but really, just making it through the Icefall was good enough for me. This was my summit and I'd had to climb past plenty of demons to reach it.

~

After clearing up my Pringles and having some rest, I headed out to film the final sequence of my trip – the triumphant return of the team. I found myself spectacularly alone and insignificant once clear of camp. The whole of the Western Cmn was empty and its silence was ringing louder than it ever had. With nothing else to do, I made myself comfortable and sat for hours meditating, dozing, remembering, and imagining.

The silhouette of a lone figure appeared from below the base of the Geneva spur and slowly descended the golden snow of the Lhotse Face in front of me. Genies of light danced all around the valley, refractions of sunshine and ice in the air, combining to make magical bundles of rainbow brightness, bobbing about like UFOs. The lone figure dissolved every now and again, behind a rock or into the brightness, and I disappeared into a world of jumbled thoughts. Each time the figure reappeared, it was a little closer, shimmering, moving with tired strides but upright and strong. Eventually there was no doubt who it could be.

Greg Paul came to a halt just short of me and stood for a moment, still swaying with his downwards momentum. He pulled his goggles off, revealing blood shot eyes, rolling around in sunken sockets. His face was gaunt and sunburnt, heavily creased with lines of experience. Flaking lips twitched for a moment before erupting upwards into an enormous rubbery grin. 'We did it, Joe!' he exclaimed and burst into tears. We hugged, with the camera squashed between us, then he staggered a few feet to the side and collapsed in the snow. He proceeded to give the most incredible account, not just of his experience on the mountain, but also pretty much of his life thus far.

He'd invested four years in this. If he had turned up and summited in 2012, he would have missed out on the rich abundance of experience, friendship and culture that had added to and shaped his life since. The summit meant a lot, but the journey had meant more, and I almost sensed a little sadness that it was now over, and he would have to start looking for a new direction.

He described crossing paths with Andreas, as he made his way back down from the summit. Andreas was still climbing up the fixed lines at the Hillary Step, with his Sherpa, Son Dorjee. The pair didn't stop to chat, but as they clambered round each other, they shared some sort of bear hug. Greg could see the whites of Andreas's eyes though his iced up googles and they stared at him with fierce intensity. 'The prayer!' Andreas shouted through the swirls of storm and continued to climb upwards.

The words spoken by Greg to God at the South Col were obviously still ringing in the German's ears, giving him extra strength and determination to continue. Faith could be a powerful fuel to burn when all else is depleted, whether you believe in God or not. This gave Greg such joy. As much, it seemed, as the summit itself. He was glowing with self-realisation and gratitude. I couldn't get a word in edgeways as he jumped from one thought to the next, but kept my camera rolling, enjoying every moment of this fine man's finest hour. It felt like a great privilege to be with him.

Andreas wasn't in quite such good shape when he eventually arrived. It was almost dark; his down suit was hanging open around him and he was clutching his right hand. Veins bulged from the side of his balding head and sweat cascaded off a very red, serious face.

On the summit, he had taken his glove off to take some pictures. Forty to fifty seconds of exposure had been enough to give him bad frostbite in his fingers. He was in a lot of pain and still had a tough journey back through the Icefall to manage, where two working hands were most certainly an advantage. The reality of this for him was dreadful, but cynically, from a TV perspective it was quite the opposite. I imagined producers back in London, rubbing their warm hands when they heard the news. That's the way this game works. People become characters, injuries become stories and decision making becomes jeopardy. My job as a producer/director is to bridge those worlds. However exciting and adventurous making TV can be, it can also be a moral minefield that, in my mind, needs to be navigated wisely and with plenty of sensitivity. As Andreas had given his full consent to be filmed throughout the expedition, my interest in his injury was fair enough.

The following morning, Andreas managed to descend the Icefall with his one working hand and, after a swift medical examination back at Base Camp, it was decided that helicopter evacuation to Kathmandu was the best option.

As the rest of the expedition team enjoyed a beer, celebrating with the Sherpa and very quickly getting quite drunk, Griber filmed the final sequence of our Everest Rescue series at Base Camp, Andreas climbing on board a Simrik Helicopter with his hand heavily bandaged. Sensing that the job was done, I chanced my luck and enquired as to whether I could join him. Surprisingly, I got the thumbs up and hastily jumped on board just as it was leaving. We flew back to Kathmandu in silence, lost in worlds of contemplation, fresh sun cream still smeared all over our beards. The wounds inflicted on Andreas by this mountain were obvious. Mine had been less so.

As we rounded the corner at Lobuche, I glanced over my shoulder towards Base Camp one last time. Would I be able to move forward, now I'd been back?

26

RUNNING MAN 5:
A MOUTHFUL OF SORREL

2020

As I turn my back on the lochan and start my run towards the
end of this book, there is a choice to be made of which direction
I go in. I could play it safe and retrace my steps or I could head
off in an entirely new direction. I can't hang around for long
though, the cold is making itself known through shivers rippling
across my goose-pimpled skin.

Each time I emerge from this lochan, I do so feeling like a
slightly better version of myself. The cold has become my friend
and I find now that a day doesn't feel complete unless I've experienced its burn. There seem to be many physical benefits to my
daily dip beyond the assistance it has given me psychologically.
Just the discipline of getting in each day feels like an achievement.
In my journey out of mind, embracing the cold has been a helpful
step. As has breath control.

Exercising my willpower over the shock of cold water and the
urge to gasp for air is a way to re-explore the moment I experienced on the glacier, as I began to suffocate inside the avalanche.
This may seem like a strange thing to want to do, but here in the
lochan, I can take back control of the process and consciously
explore what was happening to me as a result.

I have discovered that the calm witness observing my situation during that super-charged moment in Nepal and, before that, as I hung by my wrist-loop on *Don't Die*, is the same witness that I can find here, observing objectively as I override the urge to get straight out of the cold water or gasp for air. It's the same witness that must be with me somewhere, at some level, everywhere I go. This calm, objective witness has a voice of authority over the usual chittering chattering nonsense going on in my mind. This connection is easy to lose once I become aware that I have found it again. Some days it's impossible to find it at all. But other days it requires just one conscious breath to reconnect.

During those two heightened moments, there was no effort required to find it at all. The change of perspective I experienced was both overwhelming and spontaneous. I became witness to my fearful, struggling mind from a place beyond it, and it happened quite naturally. Both these experiences have left me with the sense that perhaps connecting to this objective witness is a way to connect with the infinite force of nature itself. I got a sense that it's not impossible that this connection, this change of perspective, could have vibrations strong enough to continue into the great beyond and whatever is coming next.

The change of atmosphere is noticeable as I head back inside the trees. The crunch of dead branches underfoot becomes the dominant sound as I build myself back into my flow. Life is suddenly very simple. I need to move to keep warm and I need to move well to avoid injury. This state, however primitive, is completely liberating. The more attention I give to my senses the more I am simply just here and now. A human being doing what we have done since our journey down from the trees began. Moving barefoot among them.

Tiny hoof tracks are ahead of me and Ziggy's nose twitches at fresh musk. We're off! Three wild creatures all following the same track, but all experiencing a different reality. I'm running fast and free, following and feeling, not thinking at all. I get a glimpse of a fluffy white bum as it hops over a fallen trunk and then it's gone. The roe deer has disappeared into the chaotic jumble of windfall spruce, poking out under a blanket of moss. Ziggy looks at me and wags his tail. I get on all fours and crawl after him through this soft, dark tunnel, straining my nose to smell the musk, but only picking up peat and pine. Although I seldom find myself in this position, the movement feels oddly familiar – like the rhythm to a song I recognise but don't know where from. All four limbs moving naturally in unison, hands and feet sliding through mud, hair thick with twigs, I scamper on in God knows what direction.

What I have realised as I've continued this daily routine is that it hasn't just helped me get through Post-Traumatic Stress, but that I've become happier, more grounded, and healthier than I ever have been. It's been more than a therapy to get over a difficult period, it's now a way of life. The closer I feel to nature, the closer I feel to the true nature of myself. Being able to write this book about my experiences is a result of this feeling. At times there have been tears on the keyboard as I've opened myself to experiencing these events again, releasing more emotion that I didn't realise was still within. Getting my thoughts in order on these pages, rather than all jumbled up in my head has helped me realise a crucial point.

Healing is an ongoing process. That is how to start moving forward. It's not a case of getting a certificate, ticking a box, and saying that I'm healed. It's about accepting what has happened and allowing it to become part of who I am, without it defining who I am, leaving me frozen in time.

The events that I have written about created huge waves in my psyche, taking me up and down with them along the way. Now those big waves have passed, it's about how to manage the constant flow of everyday stresses, that naturally follow on in their wake.

The stress injury I suffered may have widened the neural pathway to my fight or flight response. Because of this, I need to be more aware of how I manage my response to stress. If there is too much unmanaged stress in my system, I can usually tell. Like a hungry ghost, it will attach itself to thoughts and has the power to take me out of the present moment. An internal monologue may start, stories and scenarios created randomly. If left unchecked I can become frozen, replaying a thought over and over, decision making can become tough, and confidence can disappear. But realising this has given me some power over it.

For instance, when I see a down jacket left lying on the floor, I sometimes still experience a flashback of a dead person, particularly if one arm is left stretched out. This can kickstart the process of painful thoughts or memories. The more I try not to think about them, the more I end up thinking about them. But if I can tune in and see these thoughts from the objective perspective of my witness, the less power they seem to have over me, and the more detached I am from the emotional response they conjure. This is not always possible, but I have found the more time I spend immersed in the forest and cold water, the easier it is to find this perspective.

The insight I have gained from the extremes I have been exposed to, has helped me to realise that stress, at some level, is an ever-present force. Accepting this and learning to manage it, post-traumatic or not, is of fundamental importance to my physical and mental health.

~

Like a child engrossed in play, I follow the tracks of the deer until I don't know where I am any more. Then I delight in being lost. Ziggy is also a fan of this and, as he is very well-behaved, he would never go rogue in pursuit of a deer. Instead, he stays at my heel and is sniffing happily in all directions as we search for clues together as to where in the forest we are. What can I see through the trees? What can I hear? What do I recognise? It all looks so similar. The mental map in my mind is forever being updated with new bits of information, satisfying my deep-rooted desire for exploration. Julie is teaching yoga and it's my turn to pick Imogen and Jemima up from school, so I had better not get too lost.

I see a footprint pressed into the sphagnum sponge ahead of me and I realise that I must have been here before. That's right, this is the firebreak that leads to the badgers' set on the mound, where a red squirrel once dropped his woven nest on me from the trees above. I can see that Ziggy knows this too and has pressed ahead slightly, as if to guide me in the direction of home. 'Good boy,' I say, and he looks back over his shaggy shoulder with a wolfy grin and a wag of his tail.

I can see evidence of the badgers having fun here. Rolling around in the moss, rubbing their backs on the trees, leaving little trails of fur around polished trunks. I graze on some wood sorrel, enjoying the sweet-sour tang of its root and earthy after-taste. I think of the badgers all snuggled up underground and wonder if they can hear my footsteps. A single finger of light has pierced the canopy and is illuminating just one tree of the thousands. This beam is a back light to everything in its path, revealing in quantum detail every fibre of moss and leaf, transforming the branches into a shimmering, diamond-encrusted mosaic. Vapour rises from my breath and my body and joins with the mist rising from the trees to create a unity among us all. I stoop down to pick more sorrel – and freeze. My eye catches something unfamiliar. On the tree in front of me is a camera trap, set up for the badgers. It's pointing in my direction. I'm being filmed!

Immediately my moment of connectedness transforms into one of self-consciousness. I must have triggered it, there can be no doubt it's filming me. A wave of stress hits me. I feel my privacy has been intruded upon. I feel cross. What to do?

My mind starts racing off immediately, creating stories about how this footage of me, grazing in the forest barefoot, could be used. Will it be posted all over the internet? Have you seen this man? Will I be ridiculed? I feel I'm doing something weird again, like when I'm spotted leaving the house barefoot. And the longer I stand here, half naked, staring at the camera with a mouth full of sorrel, the weirder this situation might start to look.

ACKNOWLEDGEMENTS

This book would not have been possible without the love and support of my wife Julie. Eight years after treatment and more radiant than ever, she has encouraged me throughout this process and has always created space for me to work. Our journey together has been an eventful one, right from the off. Her patience and positivity are a constant source of strength and inspiration.

My mum, Lesley Glaister, and my stepfather, Andrew Greig, have been instrumental in writing this book. Their wisdom and insight have helped me to find my voice and given me the confidence to share it with the world. I also want to thank Andrew for allowing me to quote from his poem *Back Again* (from *Getting Higher*, Birlinn 2011). My agent, Euan Thorneycroft, was also helpful in the development of this book. He suggested I could reflect further about my mental health in the narrative and, although this was difficult to do, I am grateful to him for this suggestion. Huge thanks to my editor Moira Forsyth for her belief in this book and invaluable editorial input.

I feel blessed to have met Andy Tyson. His friendship and support during that Everest expedition will live with me forever. The Andy Tyson Memorial Fund has been set up in his memory: https://cftetonvalley.org/andy-tyson-memorial-fund/

Andy's excellent TEDx Talk from 2014 is also online. He talks from experience about the personal growth that can result from challenging yourself in the mountains and gives a detailed insight into his boulder problem metaphor for life: https://www.youtube.com/watch?v=CkOW-2ykbOA.

The support of Molly Loomis-Tyson has been imperative to this book. I am eternally grateful to her for this.

A heartfelt thank you and huge respect to Guy Cotter, Lou Dew, Anthea Fisher, Vicky Hill, Ben Jones, Sam Maynard, Greg Paul, Chhongba Sherpa, Rob Smith, Henry Todd and Rachel Tullet for taking the time to speak to me about their experiences and for allowing me to share them amongst these pages. A big thank you to Dave MacLeod and Ed Wardle for taking me with them on their adventures and to Rob Fairley for bringing me to the Highlands in the first place. And thank you to John Sutherland and Ali Berardelli for the friendship and support and to Donald Patterson, Brian Tregaskis and all my friends at Lochaber Mountain Rescue Team who are always there in times of crisis.

I am also grateful to Sam Maynard and Andrew Muggleton for providing the cover images.

Chhongba Sherpa continues with his charity work. He is chairperson for the Himalayan Tara Organisation (HTO), which works closely with the Tara Foundation USA: https://www.tarafoundationusa.org. Adventure Consultants run a Sherpa Fund which continues to support those affected by the earthquake avalanche of 2015. https://www.adventureconsultants.com/specialty-services/sherpa-future-fund/

I would like to acknowledge Grayson Schaffer's excellent article 'Everest's Darkest Year' for Outside online magazine. I would recommend it to anyone who wants further information about the 2014 disaster.

Out of Mind is the result of getting through a very difficult period of time, which wouldn't have been possible without the support and love of our friends, family and the wider community of Lochaber. There are many people, both alive and dead, who have helped me find my way and I feel tremendous gratitude to them all. And of course, thanks to the forest and Ziggy too. This book may be finished but the journey is ongoing. Peace and love.

www.sandstonepress.com

Subscribe to our weekly newsletter for events
information, author news, paperback and e-book
deals, and the occasional photo of authors' pets!
bit.ly/SandstonePress

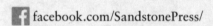 facebook.com/SandstonePress/

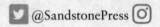 @SandstonePress